If you want to attack inequity with excellence, *Disrupting Poverty* has just the right amount of research and analysis of the concept of poverty with a magnificent primer on poverty. Above all, Bill and Kathleen give us hope and the know-how that takes all the excuses off the table.

—Michael Fullan, professor emeritus, OISE, University of Toronto

In *Disrupting Poverty,* Kathleen Budge and William Parrett offer classroom strategies while rejecting dangerous "culture of poverty" stereotypes. [And] they build a revolutionary equity framework around the strategies, equipping us with the understandings we need to advocate effectively for economically marginalized students. Budge and Parrett are two of my go-to people on poverty and education and they ought to be two of your go-to people, too.

—Paul Gorski, founder of EdChange and author of *Reaching and Teaching Students in Poverty: Strategies for Erasing the Opportunity Gap*

In this mighty book, Budge and Parrett take us beyond righteous indignation to the dark side of the moon. Here they illuminate the landscape with hope and inspiration. This is the final nail in the coffin of excuses for school failure by kids from low-income homes. ESSENTIAL reading for ALL teachers who work with students afflicted by poverty.

—Alan Boyle, coauthor *Big-City School Reforms: Lessons from New York, Toronto & London*

An excellent research-based foundation for any school staff member. As a superintendent who serves in diverse, high-poverty environments, I know this book [offers] an excellent framework to understand poverty and build an action plan to disrupt poverty.

—Tiffany Anderson, superintendent of schools, Topeka, KS

A stunning book that confronts head-on the overwhelming challenges of poverty and lays out a down-to-earth action plan. Kathleen and Bill do it with cutting-edge research from high-poverty, high-performing schools with the loud, insistent voices of real teachers. [The voices of real] teachers... call out to us, grab our attention, and move us to action.

—Bob Barr, coauthor of *Building a Culture of Hope*

Parrett and Budge's *Turning High-Poverty Schools into High-Performing Schools* transformed and focused my work with principals and teachers, leading to significant improvement in student achievement. [This book] takes their compelling message and... provides clear direction for staff who work with children in poverty. Expertly combining inspiration and practical suggestions to equip educators to take action and see results, *Disrupting Poverty* is a powerful learning tool and an essential resource in school improvement planning.

—Marian Reimer Friesen, superintendent of schools, Area 5
District School Board of Niagara, Ontario Canada

The authors challenge us to reconnect with our purpose as educators, remind us that courage comes from within, and inspire us to take action with and for our students. *Disrupting Poverty* is more than a call to action. It is a realignment of our moral compass and quite simply the right thing to do.

—Russell J. Quaglia, executive director, Quaglia Institute for School Voice & Aspirations

Educating young people who have the least ... requires us to teach as if the lives of our own children depend on our courageousness and voice—because it does. If we are intentional about addressing our biases and beliefs, we are better positioned to employ a culturally responsive approach. William and Kathleen offer readers a thoughtful and practical framework for doing just this.

—Camille Kinlock, associate director, Expanded Success Initiative, Brooklyn, NY

I grew up in poverty and found this book refreshing, thoughtful, and timely—with reason and research offering a beacon of light and hope. Includes practical classroom and personal strategies to disrupt poverty.

—Stephen R. Sroka, president, Health Education Consultants, and adjunct assistant professor, School of Medicine, Case Western Reserve University

Every educator who truly wants to touch the lives of students and improve learning should read this book. It will allow you to see through the eyes of someone who lived in poverty, as I did when I immigrated to this country, and provide you with a framework and strategies to touch the lives of your students and improve their learning.

—Maria Gonzalez, educational consultant, Miami, Florida

An easy-to-read book with facts and statistics on poverty, along with highly engaging personal stories of students and educators. [You will be given tools that compel] you to reflect on your own personal values and beliefs about poverty. The reflection questions and Application of Learning matrix could be easily used with entire staffs to push thinking and collaborative conversations around this important topic. *Disrupting Poverty* is a must read for ALL educators!

—Mary Lang, principal, North Godwin Elementary School, Godwin Heights School District, Wyoming, Michigan

A book that will pull on your heart strings and remind you why you became an educator. A powerful read that provides practical steps in addressing the issues that poverty brings to our classrooms each day.

—Taylora Schlosser, superintendent, Marion County Public Schools, Lebanon, Kentucky

Both a mirror and a map, *Disrupting Poverty* challenges educators to reflect on our own personal and historical views of poverty while providing powerful activities and practical tools to help create a more nurturing and equitable learning environment where all students can succeed.

—Mark A. Elgart, president and CEO, AdvancED

This book shines a light on five compelling practices that can make the difference between a life of freedom or a life of captivity for students who live in poverty. Through the power of story-telling, Parrett and Budge provide the essential guide for transforming a classroom, a school, a community.

—Jamey Olney, teacher, California

We can either perpetuate the damnable myth that poverty determines performance, or we can slay that beast by raising all our students to incredible heights. Parrett and Budge have yet again challenged our mindsets about the possibility—nigh, the probability—of every single child achieving at high levels. Now it's our responsibility to go out and replicate that success millions of times over.

—Pete Hall, former school principal and coauthor of *Creating a Culture of Reflective Practice*

Maya Angelou wrote, "We do the best we can with what we know, and when we know better, we do better." Budge and Parrett offer an abundance of solutions, specific tools, and options for educators to do better. All children deserve better. Let's get started.

—Michelle Krynicki, director of instruction,
Godwin Heights Public Schools, Wyoming, Michigan

William Parrett and Kathleen Budge vividly depict a wealth of innovative, practical strategies for teachers to [help] level the playing field. At the heart of their message is that the *quality* of relationships between teachers and students enables the disruption of poverty's effects on learning. This book is about transforming the culture of classrooms and deserves to be read not only by those who work in high-poverty schools, but by all who care about the practice of education.

—Shelly Wilburn, instructor, University of Cape Town, South Africa

This book demonstrates the power of individual stories. Those who tap into the personal experiences of learners for insights into keys to success, as Bill and Kathleen have here, achieve a depth of understanding about truly effective teaching and learning practices that cannot be attained in any other way.

—Rick Stiggins, assessment consultant, Portland, Oregon

Entering a classroom without this knowledge and awareness would clearly leave one vulnerable to perpetuating dangerous and erroneous stereotypes. We've got to get smarter. This book helps.

—Ivan Lorentzen, professor emeritus, 30-year school board member and chair

I loved this book and can't wait to get it in the hands of our educators. *Disrupting Poverty* is a great next step to *Turning High-Poverty Schools into High-Performing Schools*.

—Cristina Alsop, director, Title 1 Programs, Virginia Beach School District

One out of seven children lives in poverty [and is] a social issue of grave concern in Japan. Notwithstanding different social and cultural backgrounds, Japanese children are confronted with similar constraints to those in the United States. *Disrupting Poverty* is very instructive and will enhance educators' abilities. I sincerely hope teachers in Japan will acquire the ideas and methods described in this excellent book.

—Katsuhiko Yamashita, professor emeritus, Hokkaido University of Education, Sapporo, Japan

As educators we have the ability not only to disrupt the poverty cycle but also to be the conduit of hope for our children. In their groundbreaking book, Kathleen and Bill share decades of research and practical strategies and define five proven practices that disrupt poverty. A must-read book for every educator!

—Paula Kucinic, director of professional development,
Educational Service Center of Cuyahoga County, Ohio

Disrupting Poverty digs deep into this complex issue and the impact it has on children. I envision using this book as a foundational resource for facilitating professional staff development as we carve a path towards excellence.

—Krista Barton-Arnold, principal, Parkway Elementary School, Virginia Beach School District

It's not enough to be well-intentioned in our quest to educate all students to their maximum capacity. Parrett and Budge's work offers hope and strategies to help us best educate all children in our schools.

—Greg Schultz, superintendent, Oldham County Schools

This book will, without a doubt, help teachers and leaders break down the barriers that poverty creates. When I work with teachers and leaders in my district around the topic of poverty, Bill and Kathleen's research is primary in my list of recommended sources.

—Marie Verhaar, assistant superintendent, Tacoma Public Schools, Tacoma, Washington

Only occasionally does a body of work come along that not only speaks directly to the problem of situational and generational poverty in education, but also provides viable actions and responses to address the concerns with results.

—Bill Fetterhoff, superintendent, Godwin Heights Public Schools, Wyoming, Michigan

Disrupting Poverty provides a roadmap and "don't miss" stops along the way to truly disrupting the cycle of poverty in our schools, community by community, classroom by classroom, child by child. A serious practitioner's guide based on solid research.

—Donna Bahorich, chair, Texas State Board of Education

A must-have useful guide for all courageous pioneers committed to canceling out the effects that poverty can have on the lives of children... and a champion of high achievement for those who once believed their dreams of success had been deferred.

—Tracey J. Adesegun, central office administrator, Prince George's County Public Schools

Parrett and Budge have done a tremendous job of providing highly practical and extremely relevant skills and strategies that can be utilized with students across all grade and curriculum levels.

—Gail Morgan, associate executive director, professional learning,
National Association of Elementary School Principals

Parrett and Budge provide deep insight into the challenges facing schools charged with serving our most historically underserved scholars. [They] make distinct connections to research that lays a foundation for strategically developing a more aware, focused, and relentlessly committed culture for educators that will lead to increases in scholar learning and achievement.

—Kelly Mullin, chief academic officer, Wayside Schools

Growing up in a dysfunctional family with little money and behavioral issues, I found help in the alternative education programs founded by William Parrett. The one-on-one personal connections helped me succeed in school and led to my career in photography. I am thrilled Bill and Kathleen have put their ideas down on paper for us.

—Patrick A. Yockey, Michigan Majority Photographer

In *Disrupting Poverty*, teachers and administrators will find inspiration and successful strategies for improving student achievement that can be immediately implemented in their classrooms and schools.

—Rob Winslow, executive director, Idaho School Administrators Association

We were fortunate to have Parrett and Budge present an innovative approach to helping our high poverty district. Their plethora of experiences combined with an empathetic understanding of how poverty impacts education was invaluable.

—Mark R. Stratton, superintendent of schools, Corinth Central School District, Corinth, NY

I couldn't put *Disrupting Poverty* down. It is a thoughtful, relevant, and empowering book that invites professional learning and growth through reflective practice. I consider it essential reading for every professional who educates children living in poverty.

—Patricia McRae, assistant superintendent of curriculum and instruction,
Redwood City School District (retired)

Continuing the work... Bill and Kathleen's *Disrupting Poverty* shares real-life experiences where schools, following the Framework for Action, have changed the lives of their students. Each chapter provides stories and valuable insight into successfully tackling the challenge of teaching underserved populations. This latest book is as dynamic and impactful as their presentations.

—Timothy P. Sullivan, principal, Bettie F. Williams Elementary, Virginia Beach Public Schools

Disrupting Poverty dispels myths and removes excuses that impede student learning. Kathleen and Bill show compelling research and promising practices to make educating all students closer to a reality.

—Phil Gore, division director, Leadership Team Services, Texas Association of School Boards

Budget and Parrett's work empowers teachers to transform their classrooms into communities of learning where every student is an invaluable asset. This commitment to our children has never been as critical as it is today.

—Grant A. Chandler, executive director
MI Excel Statewide Field Team, Calhoun Intermediate School District

A research-based powerhouse offering salient information, self-evaluations, practical classroom tools and strategies, suggested activities for collaboration among colleagues, valuable resources, heartwarming stories of struggles and successes, and more.

—Kathy T. Glass, curriculum and instruction specialist and author

For those of us who come to work every day trying to get smarter about how to lead schools and districts for equity and excellence—and specifically, to disrupt the impact of poverty on children's learning—this book provides a gold mine of ideas, tools, and applications.

—Michael A. Copland, deputy superintendent, Bellingham (WA) Public Schools

DISRUPTING POVERTY

Other ASCD resources by the authors

Disrupting Poverty in the Elementary School (DVD)
Disrupting Poverty in the Secondary School (DVD)
Turning High-Poverty Schools into High-Performing Schools (Book)

DISRUPTING POVERTY

FIVE POWERFUL CLASSROOM PRACTICES

KATHLEEN M. BUDGE | WILLIAM H. PARRETT

ALEXANDRIA, VA USA

1703 N. Beauregard St. • Alexandria, VA 22311-1714 USA
Phone: 800-933-2723 or 703-578-9600 • Fax: 703-575-5400
Website: www.ascd.org • E-mail: member@ascd.org
Author guidelines: www.ascd.org/write

Deborah S. Delisle, *Executive Director;* Stefani Roth, *Publisher;* Genny Ostertag, *Director, Content Acquisitions;* Julie Houtz, *Director, Book Editing & Production;* Darcie Russell, *Senior Associate Editor;* Donald Ely, *Senior Graphic Designer;* Mike Kalyan, *Director, Production Services; Production Designer;* Valerie Younkin

PAPERBACK ISBN: 978-1-4166-2527-8   ASCD product # 116012

PDF E-BOOK ISBN: 978-1-4166-2529-2; see Books in Print for other formats.

Quantity discounts are available: e-mail programteam@ascd.org or call 800-933-2723, ext. 5773, or 703-575-5773. For desk copies, go to www.ascd.org/deskcopy.

ASCD Member Book No. FY18-4A. ASCD Member Books mail to Premium (P), Select (S), and Institutional Plus (I+) members on this schedule: Jan, PSI+; Feb, P; Apr, PSI+; May, P; Jul, PSI+; Aug, P; Sep, PSI+; Nov, PSI+; Dec, P. For current details on membership, see www.ascd.org/membership.

Library of Congress Cataloging-in-Publication Data
Names: Budge, Kathleen M., author. | Parrett, William, author.
Title: Disrupting poverty : five powerful classroom practices / Kathleen M. Budge and William H. Parrett.
Description: Alexandria, VA : ASCD, [2018] | Includes bibliographical references and index.
Identifiers: LCCN 2017045566 (print) | LCCN 2017056440 (ebook) | ISBN 9781416625292 (PDF) | ISBN 9781416625278 (pbk.)
Subjects: LCSH: Children with social disabilities—Education—United States. | Poor children—Education—United States. | Educational equalization—United States. | Poverty—United States.
Classification: LCC LC4091 (ebook) | LCC LC4091 .D54 2018 (print) | DDC 379.2/60973—dc23
LC record available at https://lccn.loc.gov/2017045566

27 26 25 24 23 22 21 20 19 18   1 2 3 4 5 6 7 8 9 10 11 12

To our dear friend and colleague, Scott Willison.

He dedicated his professional life to serving kids who arrived at

school with less and needed more. He always cared first about the

kids and he was a wonderful dad and husband.

We miss you, buddy.

DISRUPTING POVERTY

ACKNOWLEDGMENTS

Classroom instruction matters, and it matters immensely in high-poverty schools. This book could never have been written without the ingenuity, courage, passion, and persistence of many educators who dedicate their lives to supporting children and adolescents who live in poverty. To all of you, we owe our deepest respect and gratitude.

A specific group of talented and caring educators gave us the chance to delve into their upbringing, schooling, teaching practices, and lives as educators. Using pseudonyms to respect their anonymity, we wish to thank the very real people who shared their stories and experiences as Alex, Alva, Anna, Anton, Celia, Connie, Damon, David, Estella, James, Javon, Jon, Leslie, Lizzy, Malik, Marissa, Mary, Miranda, and Nina. Without your help, we would not have been able to examine the experiences and inner workings of highly successful educators who have supported legions of kids to overcome the pervasive adverse effects of poverty. Your incredible frankness and willingness to be vulnerable made this book possible.

We also wish to sincerely thank the district leaders and educators of Pass Christian High and Middle Schools in Pass Christian, MS; North Godwin Elementary in Wyoming, MI; Summit Charter Academy in Modesto, CA; and the Jennings School District in Jennings, MO. The educators in these high-poverty school districts opened their doors to allow us to capture on video the inner workings of their journeys to high performance and contributed numerous creative ideas that found their way into this book. We also wish to thank Ken Cornwell, Carmen Yuhas, and the ASCD film crew for their efforts to bring life to these schools' success stories.

In the past three years, we experienced the opportunity to interact with hundreds of educators in schools and school districts through extended visits to share our ideas and garner critique. Tracey J. Adesegun, Tina Alsop, Meridith Bang, Krista Barton-Arnold, Beth Bellipanni, Nicki Blake, Heidi Curry, Haleigh Cuveas, Mike Hansen, Bill Fetterhoff, Marian Reimer Friesen, Beth John, Robin Killebrew, Paula Kucinic, Mary Lang, Ivan Lorentzen, Madoda Mahlutshana, Bill McDonald, Joni Miller, Joe Morlock, Joe Nelson, Jamey Olney, Anthony Robinson, Mike Root, Tracy Sandstrom, Taylora Schlosser, Tim Sullivan, and Marie Verhaas are among the many dedicated educators who have pushed our thinking. Your experiences and insights have significantly expanded our understanding of, and appreciation for, the complexity of disrupting poverty.

We are particularly indebted to the support of so many at ASCD who have helped us with this and other related projects, beginning with Genny Ostertag, acquistions expert and our ever-present cheerleader. Genny's calming persistence, gentle support, and thoughtful guidance helped us throughout the conceptualization and writing process. A debt of gratitude goes to Darcie Russell, our editor extraordinaire whose steady encouragement, precise critique, thoughtful editing, and kindness guided this book to the presses. Darcie provided us with an encore as the finest production editor with whom we have ever had the pleasure of working. A big thank you goes to Stefani Roth, our publisher, who assisted us in ways she may not really know through her ever-present interest, smiles, and encouragement. We are also grateful to Sherida Britt, Lori Brown, Debbie Brown, Susan Race, Jim Hemgen, and Klea Scharberg for connecting us with schools and practitioners through institutes, pre-conference sessions, and other ASCD presentations that allowed us to pilot ideas and receive important and timely feedback. Finally, we extend our heartfelt thanks to the members of the ASCD Disrupting Poverty Cadre, including Tammy Alexander, Tiffany Anderson, Grant Chandler, Arelis Diaz, Margo Healy, Jay Gary, Michelle Kyrnicki, and Carmen Macchia, all of whose expertise and experience has been invaluable in supporting others to disrupt poverty.

A special word of gratitude goes to associates, colleagues, or mentors whose work informed this book in ways they may not have known, including Robert Barr, Donna Beegle, Alan Boyle, Karen Chenoweth, Michael Copland, Michael Fullan, Paul Gorski, Pete Hall, Katie Haycock, Lisa Lande, Patricia McRae, Mary Metcalfe, Dave and Clara Molden, Russ Quaglia, Roger Quarles, Joann Quinn, Rick Stiggins, Stephen Stroka, Shelly Wilburn, Katsuhiko Yamashita, and Pattrick Yockey. Each person individually influenced our work. Some pushed our thinking as scholars and others helped us with multiple connections and opportunities throughout this particular endeavor by offering ideas, creative support, and endless patience and encouragement. We are indebted to you all.

Several colleagues and friends at Boise State University were always there to support us in this effort. They include the staff of the Center for

School Improvement and Policy Studies, particularly Associate Director Kimberly Barnes, Business and HR Manager Abbey Denton, Project Coordinator Kelli Burnham, Administrative Assistant Ashley Oram, and Student Assistant Emma Thompson. In addition, we are deeply indebted to Liesl Milan, our most able doctoral research assistant who answered our calls and responded to our text messages despite the hour of the day or complexity of the request. Her support greatly contributed to the manuscript. We are also grateful for the encouragement and support of Dean Rich Osguthorpe, Associate Dean Keith Thiede, Associate Dean Jennifer Snow, and Department Chair Phil Kelly.

Finally, we are forever indebted to our close friend and colleague Larry Burke, our perpetual preproduction editor and "detail guy" who continuously improved our writing and provided invaluable suggestions for structure, format, creative adaptations, and flow.

Last and most important, we want to thank our children and their partners for their love and support: Nathaniel and Lindsey, Mia and Ahijah, Katrina and A.J., and Jonathan and Elsa.

INTRODUCTION

There is no better driver than realizing one's moral purpose.

—*Michael Fullan,* **The Moral Imperative Realized**

Disrupting poverty—does that sound like an audacious unlikely possibility? Are you skeptical? Are you hopeful? If you are either, please continue reading. Any educator who has been "in the business" for more than even a handful of years has likely witnessed the sobering increase in the number of students who live in poverty and knows an educator's job has become far more challenging as a result. The rate of child poverty is higher in the United States than in any other developed nation, and the percentage of children living in poverty continues to rise. A record number of families fell out of the middle class during the Great Recession, deepening the challenges created by poverty in urban and rural America, and increasingly in America's suburbs as well.

In 1964, President Lyndon Johnson, envisioning a Great Society, declared a "war on poverty," stating in his January 8 State of the Union address, "Our aim is not only to relieve the symptoms of poverty, but to cure it and, above all, prevent it." Today, after more than five decades of "progress" toward this goal, more than 51 percent of public students in the United States arrive at school eligible for the free and reduced-priced meals program (Suitts, 2015). In other words, more children are coming to school living in poverty than are not. We understand teachers and schools *alone* cannot "cure" poverty, or, for that matter, prevent it. We also know from studying high-poverty, high-performing (HP/HP) schools that "eliminating poverty is a *both/and* proposition—reforms must occur in *both* the broader society and in schools—*and* schools can (and do) make a considerable difference in the lives of children and youth who live in poverty" (Parrett & Budge, 2012, p. 49).

It's More Than What You Teach and How You Teach It

In *The Courage to Teach,* Parker Palmer (2007) frames a thought-provoking argument about the kinds of questions we as a nation have attended to in our attempts to improve schools. Arguing that the national dialogue is only as good as the questions it raises, Palmer explains:

- The question we most commonly ask is the *"what"* question—what subject shall we teach?
- When the conversation goes a bit deeper, we ask the *"how"* question—what methods and techniques are required to teach well?
- Occasionally, when it goes deeper still, we ask the *"why"* question—for what purpose and to what ends do we teach?
- But seldom, if ever, do we ask the *"who"* question—*who* is the self that teaches? How does the quality of my selfhood form—or deform—the way I relate to my students, my subject, my colleagues, my world? How can educational institutions sustain and deepen the selfhood from which good teaching comes? (p. 4)

As we talk about "what works" in schools, Palmer's concerns about the questions being raised continue to be relevant. In large part, our effort to "raise the bar and close the gap" continues to focus almost exclusively on the *what* and *how* questions—what shall we teach and how shall we teach it. Rarely do we ask Palmer's other two questions—*why* do we teach and *who* is the "self that teaches."

In our research into high-poverty, high-performing schools, we find the *why* and the *who* questions to be critically important. It is not that the other two are unimportant; rather, they are insufficient. Succeeding with students who live in poverty involves more than *what* we teach and *how* we teach it. What makes a teacher (and other educators) successful with students who live in poverty (and in reality, all students) requires attending to the *why* and the *who* questions. These questions implore us to reflect on our beliefs and values, as well as perhaps reconnect with our hopes, our aspirations, and the moral purposes for which we became educators in the first place. Martin Haberman (1995), who spent his career studying the difference between teachers who succeed with students living in poverty and those who don't (or who are less successful), found that the way teachers *thought about the work of teaching* and *the role of the teacher* were the distinguishing factors. In essence, he came to understand the importance of the *why* and the *who* questions because they inform the *what* and the *how* questions.

Moral Conviction Is Not Enough

On the other hand, in his profile of turn-around efforts in high-poverty schools, Michael Fullan (2011) points out that even when teachers tap into the moral dimension of teaching (the *why* question) and believe in every student's capacity to learn (part of the *who* question), they are addressing only half of the equation for success. In *The Moral Imperative Realized*, he illustrates this point through case studies of teachers in Chicago and Ontario, Canada, suggesting,

> Moral purpose without experiencing success is empty. Realization [of moral purpose] on the other hand, makes teachers *soar* because they know *how* (emphasis in original) to get success, and thus they know it can be done. They become, whenever it happens at any stage of their career, the moral agents of change that drew them to teaching in the first place. (p. 20)

We know of the transformative power of educators, particularly teachers, to improve the life chances of children and youth who live in poverty. We have seen it and felt it in many schools. True of the schools Fullan profiled, as well as schools studied by others (see Chenoweth, 2007, 2009; Shyamalan, 2013; Singer, 2014; Wong, 2011), educators in the schools we studied developed a sense of efficacy that appeared to stem from inquiry and reflection into themselves and their professional practice. What set them apart from less successful educators was *living* the four questions—*who*, *why*, *how*, and *what*—personally and collectively.

How Will This Book Help You Disrupt Poverty?

If you are a teacher, someone who supports teachers (administrator, counselor, psychologist, coach), or simply a person who advocates for all students, particularly those who live in poverty, this book will do the following:

- Help you gain deeper insight into yourself—your values, beliefs, biases, and blind spots, as well as prompt you to tap into the reasons you have chosen to do this work

• Provide you with strategies, examples, and possibilities from classrooms and schools across the country for disrupting poverty's adverse influence on lives and learning

In **Chapter 1**, we set the stage for the subsequent six chapters. First, we reintroduce the Framework for Action from *Turning High-Poverty Schools into High-Performing Schools* (Parrett & Budge, 2012), which encapsulated what HP/HP schools do, and specifically focus on the five dimensions of school culture. We suggest that those same cultural dimensions can disrupt (or mitigate) poverty's adverse influence on learning in classrooms. We describe what it means to be a proactive poverty-disrupting educator, and, to this end, we revisit the concept of mental maps to remind us of the importance of exploring the relationship between our mental map and professional practice. Next, we lay out our approach to the professional learning we are intending to foster throughout the book, including five specific tenets that are foundational to disrupting poverty. We describe how the book is designed to encourage personal reflection (to help you explore the *who* and *why* questions, in particular) and to increase your skills and knowledge (to better address the *what* and *how* questions). Additionally, we provide the Learning, Unlearning, and Relearning Summary Table (Appendix B), a tool designed to provide a model for exploring your mental map, reflecting on current practice, developing a theory of action, and planning next steps. Although the tool is presented in its entirety in the appendix, relevant sections are also provided at the conclusion of Chapters 2 through 6.

The Application of Learning Matrix in Chapters 2 through 6 will help you apply what you are learning directly to the students you teach. We strongly encourage you to use this tool, which has been field-tested with teachers. After using the matrix to answer the essential question in relationship to their students, teachers told us they were surprised and moved by what they discovered. For example, after reading Chapter 3, you will be asked to respond to the following question: *What assets, strengths, and/or cultural funds of knowledge does [insert name of each student] bring to the classroom?* Several teachers reported that although it was sometimes difficult to identify a strength or an asset in the students who most often misbehaved, they were more surprised by the realization that they did not know certain students as well as they believed they did. Interspersed between the chapters are seven profiles of teachers we interviewed. All of them have lived in poverty, and their moving stories put a personal face on poverty and how it can be disrupted.

A primer on poverty is provided in **Chapter 2**, where we urge you to think about what you know and believe about poverty—how it is defined, its magnitude, who lives in poverty, why it exists, and what can be done in schools to disrupt its adverse influence on learning. After defining poverty and reviewing the poverty rate in the United States, we examine the intersection between poverty and race, gender, (dis)ability, immigrant status, and geography. The remainder of the chapter is intended to deepen your understanding of the demographic changes many of us are experiencing in our classrooms and schools. After describing income and wealth inequity, we summarize three hotly debated theories for poverty's existence. We then describe nine poverty-related factors that often adversely influence students' lives and their readiness to learn in school, as well as information related to generational poverty in particular. This is followed by a discussion of welfare designed to address the sort of questions we often hear from educators across the country. We conclude by answering the question: What does all this mean for our students and us?

Chapters 3 through 6 present and discuss four of the Framework for Action's five dimensions of a poverty-disrupting classroom culture: (1) caring relationships and advocacy, (2) high expectations and support, (3) commitment to equity, and (4) professional accountability for learning. Creating a poverty-disrupting classroom culture is likely to require both *unlearning* and *relearning*. Most of us need to *unlearn* the myths we have acquired about people who live in poverty. Challenging such stereotypical thinking is a critical component of gaining the capacity to disrupt poverty. To support this *unlearning* and *relearning*, we provide guiding questions for personal reflection at the beginning of each chapter. We then prompt you to move from reflection to action by providing a brief synopsis of research related to each aspect of a poverty-disrupting culture, followed by practical strategies gleaned from classrooms and schools across the country. Each of these chapters concludes with suggested high-leverage questions to prompt and extend your professional learning with colleagues. Myth-busting data and research intended to question and challenge stereotypes are included in each of these chapters. In **Chapter 7** we share a few thoughts and insights about *courage and will* from the teachers we interviewed for the book. We conclude with a call upon each of us to find the courage to do what we can to disrupt poverty.

This Is Not an Ordinary "How To" Book

Disrupting Poverty: Five Powerful Classroom Practices is designed to provide not only the information, background, and practical strategies needed to disrupt poverty, but also questions, protocols, and processes for personal reflection and ongoing collaboration with colleagues. It is intended to feed your head and your heart. It is our sincere desire to remind you of how critically important you are—not only to your students, your school, and your community, but also to the very foundation of our society. We sincerely thank you for choosing to be an educator.

Are You Ready to Disrupt Poverty?

We urge you to use the self-inventory in Figure 1 as a reflection tool to gauge your learning. We recommend you complete the inventory before reading the book and again when you are finished reading.

FIGURE 1 | Are You Ready to Disrupt Poverty? A Self-Inventory

Beliefs					
Based on your personal perspective, rate/mark each statement as highly unlikely (-2), unlikely (-1), neutral (0), likely (1), or highly likely (2).					
1. Each individual's experience with poverty is unique.	-2	-1	0	1	2
2. Like any socioeconomic group, people who live in poverty are diverse in their beliefs, values, and behaviors.	-2	-1	0	1	2
3. People who live in poverty do not share a common culture.	-2	-1	0	1	2
4. Poverty adversely affects people's lives in probable and identifiable ways.	-2	-1	0	1	2
5. It is possible for educators to know and understand the adverse effects poverty has on their students.	-2	-1	0	1	2
6. People in poverty work, on average, more hours than those in the middle class.	-2	-1	0	1	2

7. Even though we have a free public schooling system in the United States, all students do not have access to an equally good education.	-2	-1	0	1	2
8. People who live in poverty value education as a means for breaking the cycle of poverty.	2	-1	0	1	2
9. Poverty is primarily caused by conditions in the broader society (including schools) that create unequal opportunity.	-2	-1	0	1	2
10. Poverty is not primarily caused by weak moral character or poor choices.	-2	-1	0	1	2

Knowledge and Skill

Based on your current level of knowledge and skill, rate/mark each statement as strongly disagree (-2), disagree (-1), neutral (0), agree (1), or strongly agree (2).

11. I can explain why my expectations of my students matter and how they influence the kind and quality of learning opportunities I provide.	-2	-1	0	1	2
12. I can list 5 ways poverty adversely affects lives and learning.	-2	-1	0	1	2
13. I can name 3–5 mindsets or practices that perpetuate inequity in the classroom.	-2	-1	0	1	2
14. I can list 3–5 ways to "level the playing field" in the classroom.	-2	-1	0	1	2
15. I can debunk common stereotypes about people who live in poverty.	-2	-1	0	1	2

Attitude/Disposition

Based on your current stance, rate/mark each statement as strongly disagree (-2), disagree (-1), neutral (0), agree (1), or strongly agree (2).

16. I am confident in my ability to successfully teach all students.	-2	-1	0	1	2
17. I am professionally responsible for the learning of each of my students.	2	-1	0	1	2
18. I make a positive difference in the lives of my students, despite the challenges many of them face.	-2	-1	0	1	2
19. I am willing to question my current assumptions and beliefs about poverty and people who live in poverty.	-2	-1	0	1	2
20. I am willing to make changes in my practice, even changes of a significant magnitude.	-2	-1	0	1	2

VOICES FROM POVERTY

ESTELLA

I grew up in a large city just outside of a really big city in the Midwest. My mother worked three shifts, so we grew up taking care of each other.

There were five of us. I was the middle child. We lived in the projects with our mother until we were able to move out when I was in the 3rd grade. I was in the first group of students who were bused in our town, and it was traumatic. On the very first day of 1st grade I stayed underneath the desk. I'd never seen so many white people in my life. It wasn't my world.

I don't know if they did that consciously, but all along the way my 1st grade teacher gave me flash cards to take home. My 2nd grade teacher introduced me to *Little House on the Prairie* books and Greek mythology.

When Dr. [Martin Luther] King Jr. died, I remember her pulling me out. I don't know that any other students were pulled out, but she pulled me out and told me to go to the 6th grade classroom so that I could watch his funeral. At the time, I had no idea the magnitude of that. Every step of the way teachers did something a little extra so that I could make it out of poverty.

The teachers allowed me to see this girl who was actually quite fascinating to me. They paired me up with some women who are now my Facebook friends, who were really my first friends who didn't look like me. I think the experience of being bused also shaped and transformed who I was. I stayed at that particular school from 1st until 3rd grade, and then in 4th grade we moved out of the projects to an apartment. I went to a school that had five people of color.

My 5th grade teacher was mean to everybody. It didn't appear to me that she liked the African Americans in her classroom. Then, when I got to middle school in January, I moved to an all-black school. That was the school where I taught my teacher how to do long division. We would have to do our classwork and share it with our teacher. When I would go up to share, he would say mine was wrong, and I would tell him his was wrong. I would just have to show him how I did my work, and then he would redo his work and tell me I was right. That happened several times.

So from 1st grade to the first half of 5th grade, all I knew was integration, and I was always the minority. Now everybody looked like me.

When I went to middle school, I had a principal who wouldn't let me get away with anything. He sat me in his office often and said to me, "Young lady, you're going to be somebody; you're going to make a difference."

I just always had teachers who believed in me. My two older brothers didn't get that experience; they didn't get that pushing and prodding.

In those "Introduction to Education" classes, they ask you the question "What teacher made a difference in your life?" As I reflected, it was because of my teachers—let me say my mother first—but certainly my teachers, who said, "OK, there's something special about this girl. Let's help her make it out."

Now that I'm involved in educating teachers, I share statistics that point out that too often the less-proficient teachers are located in the schools where the students need the most help. I didn't know that was what I was witnessing, but I lived that firsthand.

Growing up, my mother was the true example of courage. For a person who worked and did not have the language and the resources to be able to go to school, she was the person who always fought for us. And not necessarily always in the most positive way because of the skills she had at the time. But she was the person who said, "OK, not only do my children need better, but all children."

I think in every school we went to—at least the schools that were of color—she started the PTA. She was the first African American to run for the school board in our home town because she knew that things needed to change. And all this is from a person who eventually went back and got her GED. She didn't win the school board election, but it took courage to step out. The single mother in the '60s saying, "You're going to do right by my children." That's my best example of a person with courage. ■

CLASSROOM CULTURES THAT DISRUPT POVERTY

On a chilly spring day, Mr. Johnstone, a veteran high school teacher of 10 years, walked into his second-period classroom to find Elysa typing furiously on the keyboard in front of the computer he made available for any student who needed to use it. The computer was connected to a printer he kept stocked with paper, as he knew many of the school's students did not have a computer or a printer at home.

Elysa was crying as she typed. After he asked her, "What's up?" she explained: "I had a homework assignment in my social studies class I was supposed to do over spring break. I got it done, but we don't have a computer or printer at home, so I wrote the assignment in my notebook. We were supposed to summarize six current events. I did. I used my phone to look them up, but I couldn't get them typed up and printed." Mr. Johnstone asked, "And you couldn't get into the school over break to use this computer, could you?" "No," replied Elysa, "and I couldn't get to the downtown library because my mom's car isn't working and there isn't a bus, and I had to take care of my brothers most of the hours it was open."

She continued: "Mr. Walther said the best I can do is half-credit, and that is if I can get it to him typed up by the end of the day." Later in the day, Mr. Johnstone decided to talk with Mr. Walther to see if he would make an exception. After all, he reasoned, Elysa had done the assignment—wasn't that what was important? After discussing Elysa's case, Mr. Walther remarked, "Johnstone, you're such a bleeding heart. I am trying to teach these students responsibility. Other kids have it just as bad as Elysa, or worse, and they managed to get their assignment typed and printed. No, I am not making an exception. I would be doing Elysa a disservice. Someone has to teach her responsibility. She'll be out in the real world soon. No one is going to make exceptions for her there."

—*From a high school in New York*

Elysa's family income hovers around the poverty line. Living in poverty presents multiple challenges for students as they strive to keep up with the demands of school and the achievement of many of their more advantaged peers. Too often these challenges are not well understood by middle-class educators. In this case, Elysa's efforts to get her assignment done (which *poverty-disrupting* educators would likely consider both creative and praiseworthy) were overshadowed by her teacher's insistence that it was not only social studies he needed to teach her, but also personal responsibility. Does Elysa need to be taught to be responsible? Perhaps Elysa could teach many adults what it means to be responsible, given the heavy load she carries to support her family. If Mr. Walther wants to teach responsibility, should he conflate responsibility with mastering the content in terms of grades? Is such a grade an accurate reflection of what Elysa has learned in her social studies course?

As teachers and educators, we have an extraordinary opportunity to influence the course of our students' lives and the future of the country. Disrupting poverty requires us to depart from our comfort zones, to ask the hard questions, and to examine not only our individual professional practices, but also our collective practices and the classroom and school conditions that create inequities.

Our previous book, *Turning High-Poverty Schools into High-Performing Schools* (Parrett & Budge, 2012), was the result of exploring and analyzing success stories from high-poverty, high-performing (HP/HP) schools throughout the country. Out of this study, we created a Framework for Action reflecting the work of HP/HP schools (see Figure 1.1).

The framework is intended to jumpstart educators' thinking about ways they could better meet the needs of their own students who live in poverty. In these schools, administrators and teacher-leaders took action to (1) build leadership capacity, (2) focus on three types of learning (student, professional, and system), and (3) foster healthy, safe, and supportive learning environments. As a result of their actions in these three arenas, the schools' culture became more responsive to the needs of students who live in poverty, in turn raising achievement.

In each school we visited, we could literally "feel" the culture within a few minutes of stepping on the school grounds. These were places where people (adults and students) authentically felt they belonged, had a purpose, were empowered and supported, and knew they were safe. As we talked with teachers, administrators, and others, we began to understand why this was so. Educators spoke of the importance of forming caring relationships with students, holding high expectations for them, ensuring equity, assuming professional responsibility for student learning, and challenging both themselves and the status quo. In addition to these values and actions, they also shared their beliefs about their students, themselves, how they established priorities, and the way they "did business" in their schools. What they were making explicit as they shared their thoughts with us was their school's significantly improved culture.

FIGURE 1.1 | A Framework for Action

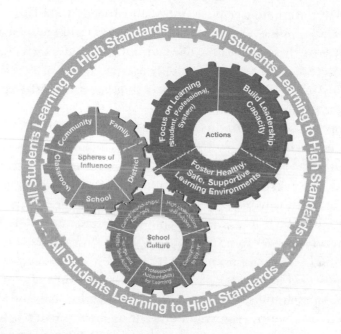

Source: From *Turning High-Poverty Schools into High-Performing Schools*, (p. 55), by W. H. Parrott and K. M. Budge, 2012, Alexandria, VA: ASCD. Copyright © 2012 by ASCD.

Culture as Values, Beliefs, and Norms

Have you ever paused to consider what constitutes school culture? When we talk about a school having a particular kind of culture, such as a *supportive* culture, a *responsive* culture, or a *toxic* culture, what do we mean? Most of us do not often analyze what we mean by culture; rather, we just know it when we see it, hear it, and feel it. School and classroom cultures are composed of values, beliefs, and norms. Values are those elements we believe to be important, and they form the foundation for a system of beliefs. Both beliefs and values are made evident in our norms or actions (Gruenert & Whitaker, 2015).

This book is about proactively creating *poverty-disrupting* classroom and school cultures. What do we mean by this? To answer the question, we first drew from our observations and experiences in the HP/HP schools we have studied. In these places, caring relationships, high expectations and support, a commitment to equity, professional accountability for learning, and the courage and will to take action exemplified what was most important. In essence, these five values formed the basis for a set of beliefs that underpinned the schools' norms (see Figure 1.2).

Based on what we learned from HP/HP schools, we turned to two groups of experts to better understand how such cultures were fostered in individual teachers' classrooms. We also sought to gauge what, if anything, might be different from, or missing in, our observations of schoolwide culture. One group was composed of preK–12 teachers (or former teachers) who were identified primarily through their supervisors or others who knew their professional capabilities. They were recommended to us because of their demonstrated success in meeting their students' needs year after year, especially students who live in poverty. These teachers, their supervisors informed us, create classroom cultures where both they and their students thrive. They are the teachers whose students routinely come back to visit and thank them for "making a difference" in their lives. In some cases, these teachers were referred to as a "kid whisperer" kind of teacher.

The other group was composed of effective preK–12 teachers who had grown up living in poverty. We were curious about the advice and wisdom these teachers could offer based on personal experience. We anticipated that their lived experiences and wisdom would be revealing, insightful, and valuable.

We recruited both groups from throughout the United States. Rather than use their real names, we have created pseudonyms for each of the educators we interviewed to protect their identity. These educators graciously shared their insights, experiences, stories, and lives with us, and now we do the same with you as the reader. Figure 1.3 lists their names (as pseudonyms) and a few other demographic details about each of them.

FIGURE 1.2 | School and Classroom Cultures in High-Poverty,
High-Performing Schools

Values	Examples of Beliefs	Examples of Norms
Caring Relationships	Caring relationships are necessary if significant learning is going to occur.	Teachers are intentional about fostering relationships with their students in all aspects of their daily work.
High Expectations and Support	All students are capable of meeting high standards when appropriately supported.	Teachers have empathy for students and an understanding of the challenges they face, hold them to high standards, provide the appropriate supports to succeed, and value the importance of effort.
Commitment to Equity	An *equal* opportunity to learn requires equitable conditions for learning.	Teachers differentiate their support based on the needs of individual students and do all they can to "level the playing field" in their classrooms for every student.
Professional Accountability for Learning	Teachers are responsible for student learning.	When students fail to learn, teachers go "back to the drawing board." They view themselves as "being on the same team" with their students.
Courage and Will to Take Action	Barriers to learning are difficult, but not impossible, to eliminate.	Teachers confront their own biases and blind spots, as well as work to eliminate conditions that perpetuate underachievement in their classrooms, schools, and districts.

In addition to the one-on-one interviews, we drew upon focus-group interviews we conducted in four high-performing/high-poverty schools during the 2015–16 school year. In total, approximately 40 educators helped us to better understand and clarify what it means *to disrupt poverty* in the classroom. Through deeply personal reflections on their work, they

FIGURE 1.3 | Educators Interviewed

Name	Teaching Level	Years of Experience	Race/Ethnicity	Gender
Alex	Middle School	14	White	Male
Alva	Elementary	8	White	Female
Anna*	Elementary	4	White	Female
Anton	High School	23	White	Male
Celia*	Elementary	13	Latina	Female
Connie*	High School	13	White	Female
Damon*	Elementary Teacher/Principal	9	Multiracial	Male
David	Elementary	5	White	Male
Estella*	Elementary/College	20	African American	Female
James	Middle School Teacher/Principal	19	White	Male
Javon*	Elementary Teacher/Principal	14	African American	Male
Jon*	Middle School	14	White	Male
Leslie	Elementary	10	White	Female
Lizzy*	High School	7	African American	Female
Marissa*	Elementary	8	Latina	Female
Mary*	High School	22	White	Female
Miranda*	Elementary	7	Latina	Female
Nina*	High School	16	Latina	Female

Note: All names are pseudonyms. An asterisk indicates an educator who grew up, or lived for a period of time, in poverty.

shared what they believe, what they value, and as a result, what actions they took to develop and sustain classroom cultures where all students could succeed. Their wisdom and advice, as well as practical strategies, are interspersed throughout this book.

What It Means to Be a Poverty-Disrupting Educator

According to the *Cambridge Dictionary*, to disrupt is "to prevent something, especially a system, process or event, from continuing as usual or as expected." This is what poverty-disrupting educators do—they create classroom cultures that mitigate the "usual or expected" adverse effects of poverty on students' learning. They do this by being proactive. Our definition of *proactive* is much more than the opposite of *reactive* or being preemptive. It is consistent with the notion Steven Covey (1989) suggested in his book *The Seven Habits of Highly Effective People.* To be a proactive person, he wrote,

> means more than merely taking initiative. It means that as human beings, we are responsible for our own lives… Look at the word responsibility—"response-ability"—the ability to choose your response. They do not blame circumstances, conditions, or conditioning for their behavior. Their behavior is a product of conscious choice, based on values… Proactive people are driven by values—carefully thought about, selected, and internalized values. (p. 39)

Teaching is values-based. There is no way around the fact that teaching is not a neutral act. This is, in part, why answering the *who* and *why* questions are a vital part of this work. One of the most difficult aspects of disrupting poverty is recognizing the barriers to learning in our classrooms and our schools, particularly those barriers that exist in our own minds—our beliefs, biases, and blind spots that form our mental map related to people who live in poverty.

The Role Our Mental Maps Play

Our mental maps are the stories, assumptions, and personal perspectives we hold about people, institutions, and the way the world works in general. They are the foundation for the theories that guide our action (Argyris & Schön, 1974). Mindsets are a part of our mental maps. The term *mindset*, as used by Carol Dweck (2010), refers to the beliefs people hold about intelligence. She identified two sets of beliefs: intelligence that is fixed (or static) and intelligence that can be grown (or developed). We know many people use the terms *mindset* and *mental maps* interchangeably; however, when we refer to mental maps we are talking about a broader concept of which mindset (as defined by Dweck) is a part. As humans, we tend to reject information that conflicts with or contradicts our mental maps; as a result, our maps are difficult (but not impossible) to challenge and change.

To illustrate, we urge you to pause in your reading and make a list (in your head, on a mobile device, or on an "old school" piece of paper) of the beliefs many people in the United States hold about people who live in poverty. Does your list include any of the following?

- Lazy or poor work ethic
- On welfare or taking advantage of "the system"
- Less intelligent than people with more wealth
- Find little value in education, including their children's education
- Abuse drugs or alcohol, or both
- Are in poverty by choice

It may or may not surprise you to know that educators throughout the United States provide a similar list of attributes whenever we ask the question. Such stereotypes are deeply entrenched in our society, and if we have lived in the United States for any time at all, it is quite likely these stereotypes have influenced our mental map regarding people who live in poverty. For many of us, separating stereotypes from reality entails the complex and difficult work of challenging our mental maps.

Disrupting poverty and proactively creating classroom cultures where all students thrive often require us to eliminate long-standing, unquestioned classroom and school practices, structures, and policies that perpetuate underachievement for students who live in poverty. To do this, we may have to confront our own mental maps related to what schools are for and how they should operate.

For example, each of us is likely to hold a distinct perspective regarding whether we should assign homework, give students "second chances" to take tests, or accept late assignments. We may debate what grades really mean and have strong beliefs about how students should behave. We also may question how much "voice" students should have in their own learning and assessment.

Our mental maps concerning what it means to be a teacher must also be considered. Do you view yourself as an advocate for children and their families who live in poverty, or do you see advocacy as beyond your scope of work? In terms of learning the content you teach, are you on the "same team" as your students in the endeavor, or are you on opposite teams? Do you often assume the role of mentor and guide for purposes far beyond learning the content you teach? When did you last reflect on why you became a teacher, and could you articulate your response in a few words?

Learning, Unlearning, and Relearning

Confronting and eliminating barriers to learning requires us to challenge our mental maps related to poverty, people who live in poverty, schooling, and what it means to be a teacher. Educators are more likely to change their conceptions if they are (1) allowed to articulate their prior conceptions, (2) provided with alternative ideas, and (3) supported to explicitly consider the status of competing ideas within their mental maps. Although competing ideas may cause cognitive dissonance—an uncomfortable sense of inconsistency or conflict with existing beliefs—that discomfort alone is not likely to change our minds and hearts. Alternative ideas "must be at least as intelligible, plausible, and/or fruitful" as the conceptions they are meant to modify or replace (Larkin, 2012, p. 26).

Throughout this book, you will have the opportunity to reflect on your mental maps and consider ideas that come from research and practice, which we are confident you will find "intelligible, plausible, and/or fruitful." This reflection and reconsideration is not easy work. Many, if not most, educators who disrupt poverty have come to understand that much of what they had "learned" about people who live in poverty was based on stereotypes and false assumptions. By confronting their own biases and blind spots, they "unlearned" and "relearned" the difference between myth and reality related to poverty.

For example, consider Ms. Taylor, a science teacher at a middle school in the Midwest, who presumed Patrick's parents did not care about their son's education because they never attended a parent-teacher conference and did not return phone calls. After a home visit accompanied by the assistant principal, Ms. Taylor learned Patrick's mother was a single mom raising three kids by herself and working two jobs Monday through Friday beginning at 10 a.m. and ending at 11 p.m., and then working another six hours on Saturday. Missing work might mean losing a job. She also learned that Patrick's mom cared deeply about his schooling, as she had only made it through junior high school herself. Ms. Taylor emerged from the visit with a changed perspective about Patrick, his mother, and the challenges poverty posed for the family. Rather than viewing Patrick's mom as an adversary, Ms. Taylor now views her as a partner she better understands how to relate to and work with.

Learning as a Social Enterprise That Shapes Professional Practice

We approach professional learning as a social enterprise—such learning occurs "in the relationship between the person and the world" (Wenger, n.d., p. 2), and it involves both individual and collective aspects. Our professional practice is shaped when we actively come to understand the meaning of our experiences in pursuit of a common purpose with others. This is what it means to learn in and through a community of practice (Wenger, 1998).

This conception of learning is also viewed as an identity-making process, not simply a cognitive exercise. It envelops the "whole person, with a body, a heart, a brain, relationships, aspirations, all the aspects of human experience in the negotiation of meaning… [it] is not just acquiring skills and information; it is becoming a certain person" (Wenger, n.d., p. 2). Moreover, becoming that "certain person" is a contextualized process where what is important to know becomes a part of what Wenger (n.d.) calls a "regime of competency" within a community of professional practice. In this case, we are defining one aspect of the "regime of competency" as the capacity to disrupt poverty, which rests on five key tenets:

Tenet 1: People's experiences of poverty are diverse.
• Although usual (or typical) patterns of adverse effects of poverty on lives and learning can be identified, each individual's experience of poverty is unique.

• We should not assume that all students (and their families) experience poverty in the same way.

• Like any socioeconomic group, people who live in poverty are diverse in their beliefs, values, and behavior.

Tenet 2: Poverty adversely affects people's lives and students' learning in probable and identifiable ways.

• Educators can know the adverse effects poverty has on their students and proactively work to disrupt (or mitigate) those effects through their daily practice.

• There is no specialized set of instructional strategies designed to specifically meet the needs of students who live in poverty. Good teaching for all students is good teaching for students who live in poverty.

• Caring relationships with each student serve as the basis for understanding each child's unique assets and challenges.

Tenet 3: Inequitable conditions in schools and classrooms further disadvantage students who live in poverty.

• Although public schools are called upon to be the great equalizer, they are also criticized as reproducing the same injustices found in society at large.

• Educators can identify and proactively work to eliminate inequitable conditions in their classrooms and schools.

Tenet 4: Educators must have the knowledge and skills (ability) to recognize the conditions that too often deny students in poverty equal access to the educational opportunities provided their more affluent peers, and the disposition (willingness) to address and correct those conditions.

• In addition to caring relationships, the keys to disrupting poverty in classrooms and schools include holding high expectations, committing to equitable practices, taking professional accountability for student learning, and having the courage to challenge one's beliefs and the inequities in the system.

Tenet 5: Stereotypes about people in poverty are deeply embedded in our society and influence our mental maps.

• Such stereotypes become part of our mental maps regarding people who live in poverty. This is important to recognize because our mental maps guide our attitudes, beliefs, and actions, as well as limit our willingness to change.

• A willingness to "turn to wonderment" (rather than judgment) and challenge our mental maps is foundational to disrupting poverty.

Labels, Stereotypes, and Deficit Perspective

Social class is only one aspect of identity. Moreover, this identity marker is dynamic. Expressing a view that was true for many of the teachers we interviewed, Nina told us,

> when I reflect back, I don't feel like I ever thought I lived in poverty. We always had clothes to wear, we always had food on the table, and then we always had meat. My dad was big on meat, so we always had meat on the table. Growing up the way I did, I never felt like I was poor. I think in the school system, that is where I started to see a different type of treatment, if that makes sense.

It is likely that many children who live in poverty have not placed a value judgment on their situation or named it as "poverty," particularly if they are young—it is simply what they know. Class-based identities are something we learn, and in large part, children first learn them in school.

How we think about and refer to our students is an important consideration. We (Bill and Kathleen) do not use the term "children *of* poverty." Rejecting the "culture of poverty" notion, we understand children to live *in* poverty, which is quite different than being *of* it. What is the opposite of *in*? *Out*, of course. What is the opposite of *of*? We are not sure, but we are certain it isn't *out*. You may think we are splitting hairs here; however, words are powerful, and they often can perpetuate or challenge our beliefs. Have you ever thought about the various ways we describe our students who live in poverty—*Title I kids, free and reduced-priced meals kids, low-SES kids, high-poverty kids*, or *poverty kids*? What do we mean when we use these labels? What is a "high-poverty kid"? What do the kids and others think when they hear these terms?

Most people in our society have a limited understanding of poverty and its history. As discussed in Chapter 2, poverty is often ill defined, and the concept is more complex than we might think. The systemic and institutional barriers to upward mobility in the United States are largely unknown to most people, including those who live in poverty (Beegle, 2007, p. 57). Paul Gorski asserts that because we do not have a good understanding of what it means to live in poverty, "we use stereotypes to fill in the blanks" (2012, p. 303).

Humans tend to view their own group identity (social, cultural, economic, racial) as being diverse while at the same time seeing "others" as more homogeneous. We are also disposed to attributing more positive characteristics to groups we identify with than those we do not. Our stereotypes are only partly a result of our own experiences. They are also the consequence of what we have been "taught" to think about others (Gorski, 2012).

Maintaining, rather than unpacking, stereotypes about people who live in poverty perpetuates deficit thinking. In their article "Pathologizing the Poor: Implications for Preparing Teachers to Work in High-Poverty Schools," Kerri Ullucci and Tyrone Howard (2015) argue that "deficit-ridden" conceptions of people who live in poverty are "consistent with the medical term *iatrogenesis*." They explain:

> Iatrogenesis refers to the phenomenon by which patients become worse after being diagnosed for medical care, through negligence or effort. In other words, the very diagnosis, which was designed to improve or cure a particular ailment, contributes to the problem becoming more severe. (p. 179)

They suggest that questioning the stereotypes we hold can "disrupt the educational iatrogenesis" that does nothing to "alleviate the challenges of poverty, but instead intensifies the constraints" we place on our students (and ourselves). "By applying the diagnosis of 'poor,' teachers often further wound the patient, rather than provide for a meaningful remedy" (p. 179). Labeling our students "poor" can provide an excuse for holding low expectations, lead to "blaming" them for their living circumstances, and contribute to a self-defeating prophecy for ourselves in terms of our ability to teach them.

Striking a Balance Between Theory and Practice

In this book, we attempt to strike a balance between theoretical work on poverty that is well conceptualized and thought provoking but, in Paul Gorski's words, "never quite manages to describe how on-the-ground educators can help to create the change" needed, and the "uber-simplistic practical solutions" that purport, but fail, to solve the "super complex and misunderstood problems" poverty poses (2013, p. 3).

Before launching into a discussion of the attributes of classroom cultures that disrupt poverty and the actions educators take to build such cultures, we begin with a primer on poverty in Chapter 2. But before you continue reading, we urge you to find a colleague or group of colleagues with whom you can extend your learning. One trait that distinguishes high-performing, high-poverty schools from low-performing, high-poverty schools is the level of collaboration between the professionals in the school. You can make a difference in your own classroom with your students, but you will make a far larger difference and find the work energizing rather than exhausting if you learn and take action with others. We encourage you to begin building or expanding your own support network by discussing the questions that follow. We hope you will also talk about ideas, insights you have gained, or questions that have arisen from what you have read thus far.

 COMMUNITIES OF PRACTICE:
Extending Your Learning with Others

- To what degree does our school embody the five values that serve as the foundation for school culture in high-performing, high-poverty schools? Provide examples.
- What might it look like to work together to disrupt poverty in our school? Describe a time when we, as a school faculty and staff, considered, interrogated, or challenged our mental maps regarding poverty.
- How do the five guiding tenets of disrupting poverty challenge our thinking?
- What might we, as educators, consider an example of "unlearning?"
- What might we, as educators, consider an example of "relearning?"

VOICES FROM POVERTY

NINA

I could read well by kindergarten. By 1st grade, I was at a 6th grade reading level. I pretty much taught myself how to read; it was my pastime growing up, and even now, it's still one of my favorite things to do. I remember getting pulled out and being put in special classes simply because I was Mexican. I didn't need to be in reading classes. That was a waste of the instructor's and my time; but I was shy, so I did what I was told.

I think in school I was quickly classified because of my cultural background. With that came multiple other stereotypes: that you're poor; that you get no support at home; that your parents don't care about your education.

Growing up, I never felt like I was poor, but we did work our butts off. We worked in the fields every summer. Even when I was too young to do it, I remember hanging out on the side, playing in the ditches and the canals, waiting for my family to work the full day.

Anything that we did growing up was to earn money to help sustain the family. It wasn't something that was for our pocket or to prepare for college or to save or to buy ourselves anything. We would work in the fields, get our paycheck. My parents would hand it to us with a pen; we would sign the back and we would hand it right back.

I never felt like something was wrong or was being taken away from me. I just always knew that any work that I did was to help provide for the family. When you're having your seven children help maintain the family to help keep food on the table and clothes on our backs, that is poverty status.

From early on, my mom and dad raised us in a family that was very sheltered. We weren't allowed to date and weren't allowed to go to dances unless my brother was with us. That never changed until we left home. I didn't feel like we were raised badly, just strictly. Unfortunately, some of my other siblings chose to make poor decisions. I have a brother still in prison and others who have struggled.

In 4th grade, my teacher was getting on my parents about my attendance. I got really sick at one point and missed multiple days. My teacher thought that my parents were keeping me home to take care of my younger siblings, which, in all honesty, I had done a couple of times. Back at school, I had medication that I had to take, and I remember her hovering over me to see if I really was going to take the medication. She didn't believe that's why I missed.

I remember being under the microscope when I was younger and having to go to those special classes; that was negative to me as a Hispanic child. But I was always smart; I was a 4.0 student all the way through junior high, all the way through high school and I never struggled academically, but at certain points I really felt like I was under a microscope, like almost a little too hard, especially since I was a really good student. I was never a disruption problem. I really didn't need a thumb on me. It's like, "Where is this coming from?"

Yet for some reason, for as long as I can remember, I've always wanted to be a teacher. There's nothing that could have ever steered me in any other way. Despite the challenges, I always loved going to school. When my mom went back to school, I really loved going to class with her. All my brothers and sisters, we would fight over who was going to go to class with Mom. The deal was we just had to sit quietly out in the hallway with snacks and a book, or we could sit in the classroom, but we couldn't make a peep. We had to listen or do our own thing and keep ourselves entertained. I'm sure that was probably a huge influence on me too.

Living that way, or being raised that way, I never thought I wouldn't go to college.

An assumption that a lot of people make is that children from poverty don't ever think of college as an option. I think it's because of my mom's influence. I never thought the opposite. ■

2 | A POVERTY PRIMER

I have always lived on the other side of the tracks, whether it was the rural isolation of small prairie towns in the upper Midwest where I was the only individual of color in a town of 12,000, or the urban extreme of six different big cities. I never lived in the same house for more than two years, never attended the same school for more than three years, or stayed in the same state for more than four. There was never any mention of the importance of academic grades, degrees, or hard work from my parents, foster parents, grandparents, or any others in my family. I worked full-time jobs almost as long as I can remember, even before I was legally old enough, just to support myself. I never had the lifestyle or security a decent parental income can provide. As I think back, my prospects for even getting to high school were dismal, confirming a fate that I had accepted early in my youth It's really hard to change circumstances dealt to you as a child, or erase a history of indifference and neglect.

Malik, describing his experience of growing up in poverty In America

 ## ANSWERING THE "WHO" QUESTION:
A 100-Word Reflection

Adults learn best when their personal experiences are combined with reflection as a starting point (Knowles, 1980; Kolb, 1984). Paulo Freire, noted scholar of literacy (1970), stressed the importance of actively engaging learners in a process of reflecting not only on the *literal text* they were reading, but also on the *text of their lives*. This chapter, and each of the next four chapters, begins with a question to prompt you to write a 100-word reflection to jumpstart your learning. We became familiar with the power of 100-word reflections from a colleague who uses this technique with teachers in England, and we urge you to "give it a go."

Where do my ideas about poverty come from? _____

_____

_____

_____

_____

ANSWERING THE "WHAT" QUESTION:
What Research and Policy Tell Us

In this book, we make poverty and the inequities that are related to socio-economic class our primary focus for three reasons. First, discussions of poverty, socioeconomic class, and classism tend to get marginalized in broader considerations of social justice. Growing up in generational poverty, Donna Beegle (2007), whose family members were migrant farmworkers, describes poverty as "the unspoken diversity issue" (p. 145). We agree with her call for poverty "to be placed at the center of our struggle as a society toward achieving equity and social justice" (p. 145). Other scholars assert poverty is unrecognized in U.S. society and claim, "much like the phenomenon of color blindness—a critical next move is simply unveiling the truth" (Ullucci & Howard, 2015, p. 188). Lindsey, Karns, and Myatt (2010), authors of *Culturally Proficient Education: An Asset-Based Response to Conditions of Poverty,* declare poverty "must be a visible topic in our schools." They suggest, "Considering socioeconomic issues separate from other demographic groupings provides educators with the opportunity to accurately assess needs and develop programs" (p. 15). We are not arguing that considerations of classism are more important than other forms of discrimination. Children who live in poverty often have fewer opportunities to access a high-quality education than their more affluent peers, and those who are children of color are often confronted by multiple forms of discrimination and marginalization.

Second, poverty is complex, and misunderstandings about it abound. Paul Gorski's books and articles have shed important light on some of these misunderstandings (see "The Myth of the 'Culture' of Poverty," 2008).

Poverty's complexity requires a concentrated focus on the issue. In the words of Ullucci and Howard (2015), "Poverty has long tentacles and interjects itself in all manner of ways" (pp. 187–188). Throughout this book we describe many of those ways—as well as how educators respond.

Third, as a country, the United States is losing ground in terms of providing all students with an equal opportunity for access to a meaningful education. In their book *Restoring Opportunity: The Crisis of Inequality and the Challenge for American Education,* Duncan and Murnane (2014) report on a study that assessed students' reading and math skills just after they began kindergarten and again in 5th grade. Comparing children from families in the top 20 percent income bracket with those from the bottom 20 percent, they found children from affluent families had an advantage of 106 percentage points in early literacy at the beginning of their schooling experience. Furthermore, "this gap is nearly equal to the amount that the typical child learns during kindergarten" (p. 25), and the gap was even larger when the students were assessed in 5th grade. Some scholars claim that poverty, more than other variables, can explain gaps in academic achievement (Anyon, 2005; Rothstein, 2004).

What Is Poverty?

Poverty is complex, beginning with how we define it. "Poverty in its most general sense is the lack of necessities. Basic food, shelter, medical care, and safety are generally thought necessary based on shared values of human dignity" (Bradshaw, 2006). However, poverty is also thought to be relative to the social context in which it is experienced. Valentine (1968) asserts, "the essence of poverty is inequality. In slightly different words, the basic meaning of poverty is relative deprivation" (as cited in Bradshaw, 2006, p. 4). The most common, and in the United States, perhaps the most "objective" definition for poverty is the statistical measure established by the federal government.

Poverty by the Numbers

In the United States, the federal government defines poverty as a certain level of income relative to family size. For example, in 2016, the poverty threshold ranged from $12,229 for a single person to $24,339 for a family of four. Still in use today, the formula for determining who lives in poverty and who does not was created by federal statisticians based on what was determined to be three times the cost of food for a family of three in 1963! The formula is considered by many to be excessively conservative. Much has changed in our society since 1963. Yet changing the formula has proven highly controversial and political and so it remains unchanged. Based on the 2016 U.S. Census, nearly one in eight people lives in poverty, 40.6 percent of the population (Semega, Fontenot, & Kollar, 2017). To help put a human face on these numbers, you or your school may want to consider using an online poverty simulation such as the one developed by the Urban Ministries of Durham, North Carolina (playspent.org), or the face-to-face interactive poverty simulation developed by the Missouri Community Action Network (povertysimulation.net).

Child Poverty More than 13.3 million children live in poverty, or about 18 percent. Another 17 million (about 24 percent) live in families considered low-income (Semegar, Fontenot, & Kollar, 2017) Figure 2.1 depicts the annual change in the percentage of children living in poverty in the United States since 2008.

Defining Poverty in the Context of Schools Educators use a different set of numbers to define poverty in the context of schools—eligibility for the federally subsidized free and reduced-priced meal program. For the 2015–16 school year, income eligibility for reduced-priced meals was established as 185 percent of the federal poverty line and 130 percent for free meals. For example, a family of four with a gross income of $40,793 was eligible for the reduced-cost meals and if they earned less than $28,665, they could receive free meals. In 2015, for the first time since the inception of the federally subsidized meal program, the majority of fourth grade students in the country were eligible for the program.

The Geography of Poverty In many people's minds poverty represents an urban problem; nonetheless, since poverty rates were first officially recorded in the 1960s, a greater number of people living in poverty have historically resided in rural places, and since 2000, the occurrence of poverty has greatly increased in the nation's suburbs. In *Time Magazine*, Brookings Institute scholar Elizabeth Kneebone, coauthor of *Confronting Suburban Poverty in America* (2013*),* explained, "Poverty is touching all kinds of communities. It's not just *over there* anymore" (Sanburn, 2013). Figure 2.2 shows a geographical distribution of child poverty in the United States.

FIGURE 2.1 | Child Poverty Over the Years

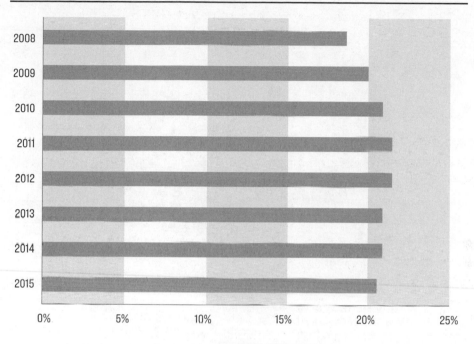

Percentage of Students Living In Poverty

Source: Data from Annie E. Casey Foundation (2017). *2017 Kids Count Data Book*. Baltimore, MD: Author.

Scholars and policy analysts suggest that to meet their most basic needs, families require about two times the federal poverty threshold (Children's Defense Fund, 2014). If you are wondering how well one might fare living at or below the poverty line in the town or city in which you live, we encourage you to visit livingwage.mit.edu. You will find a calculator developed by Amy K. Glasmeier at the Massachusetts Institute of Technology (MIT) that can be used to determine the "living wage" needed to meet a family's basic needs in your community.

FIGURE 2.2 | Child Poverty in the United States 2013

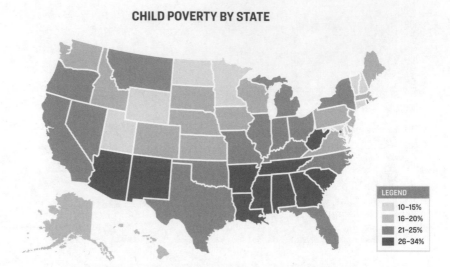

CHILD POVERTY BY STATE

LEGEND
- 10–15%
- 16–20%
- 21–25%
- 26–34%

Source: Southern Education Foundation, (2015). *A new majority research bulletin: Low income students now a majority in the nation's public schools.* © 2015 by Southern Education Foundation. Adapted with permission.

Poverty's Intersection with Race, Gender, and Immigrant Status

It is important to consider and understand the intersection between race and poverty. Figure 2.3 shows the percentage of school-age children by race living in poverty in the United States.

Understanding What Intersectionality and Disproportionality Mean

Blacks, Hispanics, American Indians, and children of two or more races disproportionately live in poverty. Picture a classroom with 24 students. If all those students were American Indian, Hispanic, or African American, chances are more than one in three would be living in poverty. If that same class was composed of all white children, one in eight would be living in poverty (Annie E. Casey Foundation, 2017).

Increasing Income and Wealth Inequity Although people tend to use the terms *wealth* and *income* interchangeably, they are quite different. *Income* is cash wages and other cash sources of earning, while *wealth* refers to the total worth of one's assets— houses, real estate, cars, furniture, bank accounts, retirement funds, stocks, etc., minus one's debts. Those at the very top of the wealth distribution usually have the most income; however, it important to note that for the wealthy, most of that income does not come from working. In 2008, only 19 percent of the income reported by the 13,480 individuals or families making more than $10 million annually came from wages and salaries (Domhoff, 2017).

FIGURE 2.3 | Percentage of School-Age Children Living in Poverty by Race

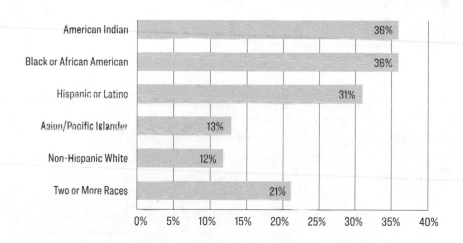

Source: Data from Annie E. Casey Foundation (2017). *2017 Kids Count Data Book*. Baltimore, MD: Author.

Income inequality in the United States is the fourth highest of the member nations in the Organization for Economic Co-operation and Development (OECD), after Chile, Mexico, and Turkey (OECD, 2011). America's wealthiest citizens have most benefited from economic gains in the past three decades, with the share of the national income of the top 1 percent doubling between 1980 and 2008. The wage gap between the richest and the poorest of U.S. full-time workers has increased by almost one-third, more than in most of the developed world (OECD, 2011). Another picture of inequity is found in how wealth is distributed. "[T]he wealthy 10% of U. S. households have captured a whopping 76% of all the wealth in America" (Ingraham, 2015).

Explanations for Poverty

Competing theories abound regarding why poverty exists. It is important to reflect on what we believe about the causes of poverty as these beliefs shape the solutions we use in our classrooms and those we will support more broadly in our schools. The three most common perspectives used to explain poverty include (1) personal-individual, (2) cultural, and (3) structural-institutional.

The Personal-Individual Perspective

Personal-individual ideology focuses on the personal character, values, and behaviors of the individual as the explanation for poverty. It is consistent with the belief that poverty is the result of poor choices and weak moral character, as well as a "lack of genetic qualities such as intelligence" (Bradshaw, 2006, p. 6). Claimed to be one of the oldest justifications, it has ties to religious doctrine (Bradshaw, 2006, p. 6) and eugenics—the concept of "inherited intelligence," which rationalized poverty as the logical consequence of people with limited intellectual ability (Bradshaw, 2006). The personal-individual perspective is consistent with economic theories that point to the welfare system as actually increasing the level of poverty by encouraging unemployment and "using the system."

Theorists say it is hard to overestimate the pervasiveness of this explanation in our society (Bradshaw, 2006). This perspective is quite prevalent among educators. In schools you might hear statements from those who ascribe to this theory, such as *Those parents are lazy and irresponsible; look how many days this student has missed this year.* The value placed on individualism in America—the Horatio Alger myth that through hard work and perseverance any individual can succeed—contributes to the deeply engrained nature of this theory.

The Culture of Poverty Perspective

Perhaps the most controversial, the culture *of* poverty perspective or theory has been widely debated for decades. This theory is sometimes closely connected to the personal-individual theory in that people in poverty are thought to "create, sustain, and transmit" a culture that reinforces their social, moral, behavioral, and intellectual deficiencies (Jordan, 2004, p. 19). Others say "individuals are not necessarily to blame"; rather, they are victims of their culture (Bradshaw, 2006, p. 8). In essence, those who ascribe to this theory believe people, by virtue of living in poverty, develop "a shared set of beliefs, values, and norms for behavior that are separate from, but embedded" in mainstream culture (Bradshaw, 2006, p. 8). This theory has been broadly and deeply researched, and although "these studies raise a variety of questions and come to a variety of conclusions about poverty... on this they agree: 'There is no such thing as a culture of poverty'" (Gorski, 2008, p. 33). Nonetheless, the culture *of* poverty theory has a significant hold on the American psyche, and, by extension, on those of us who work in schools.

Belief in a shared deficient culture as a paradigm for poverty can be heard in the question recently asked at one of our workshops: *"If the culture of poverty doesn't exist, why do they go back? Even when they have a chance to get out—you know, go to college or get a job somewhere—they so often come back, come back to what they know—to the culture of poverty."* If leaving poverty means leaving one's family, support system, social network, and home, as it often can, how many of us would like to be asked to do so? Overwhelmingly, the teachers we interviewed who grew up in poverty talked about the love, support, and encouragement they received from their families. Many of them told us it wasn't until they went to school that they realized they indeed lived in poverty, and then they did not have a name for it until they became old enough to understand the marginalized treatment and substandard education they often received.

The Structural-Institutional Perspective

From a broad structural-institutional perspective, scholars and policymakers point to the "economic, political, and social system, which causes people to have limited opportunities and resources with which to achieve income and well-being" (Bradshaw, 2006, p. 10). Capitalism, they assert, inherently results in some level of income inequality. More specifically, low-wage jobs that rarely offer benefits, a limited number of jobs near the workforce (such as in abandoned inner cities and isolated rural communities), the erosion of the buying power of the minimum wage, and job and wage discrimination based on race and gender are suggested as contributing to poverty.

Various forms of oppression (power and privilege of one group over another), such as racism, ableism, genderism, and religious bias, limit access to opportunities to combat poverty and improve life chances, with "discrimination based on race and gender... creat[ing] the most insidious obstructions" (Jordan, 2004, p. 22). Housing discrimination based on race provides one example of how certain groups of people, particularly African Americans, have been systematically denied opportunity. This practice has not simply resulted in substandard housing; it often limits access to such resources for human development as quality schools, libraries, parks, and other public services. Moreover, purchasing a home is the primary means through which the middle class increases its overall level of wealth. Those left out of this way to accumulate assets are significantly economically disadvantaged.

Testing Multiple Explanations for Poverty

Gregory Jordan (2004), in an article entitled "The Causes of Poverty—Cultural vs. Structural: Can There Be a Synthesis?" describes his statistical analysis that aimed to empirically establish the degree to which the competing paradigms (cultural and structural-institutional) were interrelated in their influence on poverty. Contrary to his hypothesis, he could not demonstrate a relationship between the cultural aspects thought to contribute to poverty (divorce, crime, teenage pregnancies, and welfare) and the structural aspects (unemployment, income, race, income inequality, gross domestic product [GDP], and incarceration). Further, none of the cultural variables had a statistically significant impact on poverty, either independently or in conjunction with the various structural-institutional variables. In other words, divorce, crime, teenage pregnancy, and welfare do not cause poverty. On the other hand, unemployment, income inequality, and the GDP demonstrated a statistically significant influence on poverty.

Poverty's Adverse Effect on Lives and Learning

Poverty poses significant constraints on the choices available to negotiate life, particularly children's lives. Many of the 13.3 million children living in poverty face food insecurity, housing instability (including homelessness and doubling-up), inadequate health care, unsafe neighborhoods (as indicated by violence and crime, and unsafe housing), and little of the necessary infrastructure (including high-quality schools, libraries, youth services) to develop their human capacities. Poverty results in multiple *intervening factors* that, in turn, affect outcomes for people (Brooks-Gunn & Duncan, 1997). The following paragraphs describe 11 intervening factors that can negatively affect children and adolescents living in poverty.

Material Resources

Poverty often constrains a family's ability to provide access to high-quality day care, access to before- or after-school care, and physical space in their homes to create an environment conducive to studying. Students in poverty may not have the resources to complete out-of-class projects, own a computer, or have access to high-speed Internet. Families may not be able to provide basic clothing such as underwear, socks, shoes that fit, winter coats, hats, boots, mittens, and so on.

Health and Well-Being

Poverty's adverse effect on health and well-being is well documented. People living in poverty often have less access to quality medical care and nutritional food. These factors affect the rate of childhood disease, premature births, and low birth weights, which in turn influence children's physical and cognitive development. Children in poverty are likely to suffer from emotional and behavioral problems more frequently than are children who do not live in poverty (Brooks-Gunn & Duncan, 1997).

Food Insecurity

Many people who live in poverty experience food insecurity. Inadequate daily nutrition impairs healthy growth and brain development, particularly in the earliest years of life. In the United States, 42.2 million people lived in food-insecure households in 2015, according to the U.S. Department of Agriculture   (https://www.ers.usda.gov/topics/food-nutrition-assistance

/food-security-in-the-us/key-statistics-graphics.aspx#householdtype).
Children in black and Hispanic households were more than twice as likely
to experience food insecurity as their white counterparts. Seventy-five percent of households with food insecurity in 2010 and 2011 had one or more
working adult, 80 percent of whom held a full-time job (Children's Defense
Fund, 2014).

Neurocognitive and Neurobehavioral Development

"Poverty has cascading effects on neurocognitive development…"
(Azma, 2013, p. 40), and the longer a child lives in poverty, or the deeper the
poverty, the greater the adverse effect (Brooks-Gunn & Duncan, 1997). Poverty contributes to problems with executive functioning, which includes
the ability to plan, self-regulate, attend to tasks, understand what information is relevant or irrelevant to a task, and retrieve and store information
over time (working memory). It also adversely affects social comprehen-
sion and regulation of emotion. The good news is the brain's *plasticity*
makes it possible to disrupt many of these adverse effects, and although
most effective in early childhood, interventions well into adulthood have
been found to be successful (Babcock & De Luzuriaga, 2016).

Housing Instability

Poverty often means families have difficulty securing stable and safe
housing. Available housing choices often can expose them to environmental toxins such as lead paint, which has a harmful effect on health and
development (Brooks-Gunn & Duncan, 1997). Poverty can also mean no
home at all. In 2013–14, more than 1.3 million students were homeless, and
approximately 76,000 students were living on their own (National Center for Homeless Education, 2016). Many students live in families that are
"doubled up" with others, such as friends and relatives. Others live tempo-
rarily in hotels or motels or spend at least some nights in cars, parks, camp-
grounds, or abandoned buildings. Homelessness is often a particularly
shaming experience that children are reluctant to disclose to their teachers
or other adults. They may fear they would be taken from their families if
others found out. In addition to the obvious adverse effects homelessness
can have on health and hygiene, these effects can also make homeless students a target for bullying (Dill, 2015).

Family Stress and Trauma

Poverty can trigger a "host of life-conditioning experiences that erode the protective capacity of the family in ways that traumatize both parents and their children" (Craig, 2016, pp. 23–24). Unstable or inadequate housing, food insecurity, limited transportation options, and neighborhood risk factors all contribute. "The result is a pattern of trauma-organized behavior that impairs family functioning..." (Craig, 2016, p. 24). Stress and trauma can adversely affect the ability to make decisions, solve problems, and set goals. It can cause people to lose hope and view their actions as futile. It can leave children with "little or no 'buffer zone' to safeguard their development" (Craig, 2016, p. 25). The stress of living in poverty can affect the level of the hormone cortisol, which inhibits executive functions important for academic success. But, there is some good news. In a news release from the National Institutes of Health (2012), Clancy Blair of New York University stated, "stress is a malevolent force," but finding ways to reduce it "can boost children's capacity to learn."

Neighborhood Risk Factors

People living in poverty are often constrained in their choice of neighborhoods. If they live in places with concentrated poverty, such neighborhoods are commonly characterized by unemployment, crime, and violence, as well as few resources for child development, such as parks, playgrounds, child care facilities, medical/health clinics, libraries, or museums (Brooks-Gunn & Duncan, 1997). One study suggests that neighborhood deprivation is similar in the size of its effect on children's developmental status as is the loss of a parent through death or separation (Caspi, Taylor, Moffitt, & Plomin, 2000). Neighborhood influence has also been linked with juvenile delinquency, drug use, conduct disorder in teenagers, and teenage out-of-wedlock births (Brooks-Gunn, Duncan, Klebanov, & Sealand, 1993).

Interrupted Schooling

Chronic absenteeism occurs at a higher rate in high-poverty schools (Balfanz & Byrnes, 2012). There are many possible reasons for chronic absenteeism among students who live in poverty, including housing instability, unreliable transportation, health problems, trauma, violence in the community, and the need to care for siblings. Students who experience long periods of interrupted schooling face some of the highest risk of failure (Walsh, 1999). When students come back into the school system after an extended absence, they tend to lack understanding of basic concepts, content knowledge, and critical thinking skills. These students lack the topic-specific languages of academic subjects and the social understanding of how to "be" in a classroom (Brown, Miller, & Mitchell, 2006).

Language and Literacy Development

Fifty years of research demonstrates that children who live in poverty often come to school behind in language development and with fewer early literacy skills than their peers. As Susan Neuman (2008) explains in her book *Educating the Other America,* such children "hear a smaller number of words with more limited syntactic complexity and fewer conversation-eliciting questions [than their more affluent peers], making it difficult for them to quickly acquire new words and to discriminate among words" (p. 5). They also have less access to reading materials in their homes (Allington & McGill-Franzen, 2008).

Social Capital

Social capital is gained by forming relationships in formal and informal social networks. Participation in such networks requires an understanding of the group's norms and gaining the group's trust (Coleman, 1987). In the United States, we tend to live very isolated lives, associating primarily with those in our own socioeconomic class. Middle- and upper-middle-class families often construct informal networks that become an asset when negotiating the bureaucracy of schools and advocating for their children. People who live in poverty (especially those whose children are in high-poverty schools) are often isolated from these networks and can be isolated from each other. Even when informal networks are in play among people who live in poverty, they may be used primarily to support each other as they deal with the daily realities of poverty rather than to tackle school bureaucracy.

Cultural Capital

Students who live in poverty often do not come to school with the same kind of class-based capital as their more affluent peers. Those peers have often been socialized to the cultural benefits of exposure to libraries, museums, theater, travel, or books on Western civilization. Such knowledge is rewarded in schools (Parker & Shapiro, 1993). Duncan and Murnane (2014) point to the growing income inequality we discussed earlier in this chapter as an important element in understanding the increasing gap between low-income and upper-income families in their ability to pay for college, as well as understanding the increasing gap in test scores between students from high-income families and those from low-income families. Upper-income parents are simply spending much more than they once did to ensure their children have experiences that contribute to their success in school. The difference in spending has nearly tripled in the past 40 years (p. 28).

Welfare: Questions and Answers, Fallacies and Truths

We are often asked by educators, what about welfare? Doesn't welfare address most of these intervening factors? As we said about poverty, a discussion of welfare is also more complex than one might think.

An important starting point is the fact that there is no program called "welfare." Multiple government-funded programs administered by various departments of federal and state governments provide benefits to individuals based on various factors to reduce poverty in the United States. Additionally, there is little consensus among policymakers, lawmakers, and scholars about which government-funded programs are "welfare" and which are not. Some argue that only those programs that require a "means test" to determine eligibility should be considered welfare. A means test considers the applicant's income in relationship to the context (things such as cost of living; debts; presence of children, elderly, or disabled in the home) to determine eligibility.

Others argue that any form of government benefit, whether in the form of "cash transfers" or tax deductions or credits, should be considered welfare. Still others make a distinction between programs to which individuals make a contribution (such as Social Security) and those that do not require a contribution in order to receive the benefit. This lack of definition contributes to the confusion surrounding government-funded support. Adding to the confusion, many terms are used as proxies for the term *welfare*, such as *anti-poverty programs*, *public assistance*, *government assistance*, *social welfare*, and *entitlements*.

Anti-Poverty Programs and Who They Serve

The U.S. Census Bureau analyzed and reported on demographic characteristics of participants in six of the larger programs from 2009 to 2012, including Medicaid, Housing Assistance, Supplemental Security Income (SSI), Temporary Assistance for Needy Families (TANF), General Assistance, and the Supplemental Nutrition Assistance Program (SNAP), formerly known as food stamps (DeNavas-Walt & Proctor, 2015). Roughly 20 percent of the population accessed these programs, with 15 percent receiving Medicaid and 13 percent using SNAP. *Only 1 percent of the population was provided cash benefits through TANF or General Assistance.* The average monthly benefit is approximately $400. Children make up the largest group of people accessing support (39 percent). About 30 percent of the recipients used the support for a year or less, and 43 percent accessed it for three to four years.

Two Fallacies About Welfare

Fallacy 1: Welfare recipients don't work. Many policymakers and politicians have long claimed that government assistance is creating an "entitlement state" where people are dependent on government for food, health care, housing, and so on, and their work ethic is destroyed. "Such beliefs are starkly at odds with basic facts..." suggest Sherman, Greenstein, and Ruffing (2012), from the Center on Budget and Policy Priorities. They reported in 2010 that 91 percent of the total welfare expenditures in the United States were directed to children, the elderly, people with disabilities, and the working poor, and the bulk of that percentage went to the elderly (53 percent). *Only about 10 percent of all welfare spending is directed to non-working adults* (Sherman, Greenstein, & Ruffing, 2012). In addition, most welfare programs require recipients to work or to document that they are seeking employment (see www.welfareinfo.org).

Fallacy 2: Welfare is not effective. Not only do some policymakers and politicians blame welfare for causing poverty by promoting laziness and dependency but they also point to increases in welfare spending as proof the programs do not work. It is true that poverty has been on the rise, dipping slightly only in 2016; however, income and wealth inequality has continued to increase. Additionally, with a stagnant minimum wage and a decreasing number of living wage jobs, it is not difficult to understand the numbers. After World War II, the poverty rate fell when the standard of living rose for the poor and middle class at a similar rate as for the wealthy. Such is not the case now, as noted in a report by the Stanford Center on Poverty and Inequality: "The primary reason that poverty remains high is that the benefits of economic growth are no longer shared by almost all workers, as they were in the quarter century after the end of World War II" (Danziger & Wimer, 2014, pp. 16–17). The report points out that "stagnant earnings for the typical worker and higher unemployment represent a failure of the economy, not a failure of anti-poverty policies" (p. 18).

"Welfare" for the Middle Class and the Wealthy

It has long been argued that all Americans receive government benefits in some form. The wealthy and the middle class benefit primarily from tax subsidies. In fact, Eric Toder and Daniel Baneman (2012) of the Tax Policy Center looked into the question of who would be most affected if individual "tax breaks" were repealed. Those with income in the lowest quintile (20 percent) would see their incomes drop by 7.5 percent; however, those in the highest 10 percent would see their incomes fall by twice as much—15 percent. Twenty-five percent of the itemized deductions are claimed by the top 1 percent, with almost none claimed by the bottom 40 percent.

Those who take the deductions for mortgage interest or student-loan interest when we file our taxes are benefiting from a government-funded program. Benefits directed toward the middle class and the wealthy are comparable in their intent and cost to benefits directed at fighting poverty. Moreover, because these benefits are "submerged" and many people are unaware or uninformed, researchers assert, they can become angry at having to pay higher taxes while seemingly getting no benefit, which in turn contributes to antigovernment sentiment and political polarization in America (Koch & Mettler, 2012).

What All This Means for Our Students and Us

Nearly every phone call or e-mail we receive from educators includes some mention of the changing demographics of their classrooms and schools. The conversation typically goes something like this: *"We used to be a very middle-class community with mostly middle-class kids. Now we have a growing population of non-native English speakers and increasing poverty. We are not sure what to do. We have tried a lot of things, but nothing seems to work."* Others are more blunt: *"These aren't the kids I was prepared to teach or signed on to work with."*

Although economic growth has been steady (the GDP has doubled in the past 50 years), as we previously mentioned, the benefits are no longer being shared by most workers, as they were in the years following World War II (Danziger & Wimer, 2014). As an educator, you are affected daily by the demographic changes resulting from this inequity. High-income families have gained far greater purchasing power, while families on the other end of the continuum have seen their purchasing power dramatically decrease.

In the past 30-plus years, communities with an agricultural base have been left out of this new U.S. economy as family farms disappear and agribusiness increasingly becomes the nation's primary mode of food production. Whether it's the closing of the Kodak plant in Rochester, New York; elimination of a General Motors stamping plant in Wyoming, Michigan; or the shuttering of Stimson Lumber in rural Libby, Montana, changes in manufacturing and in industries based on resource extraction, such as logging, mining, and fishing, have altered the economic landscape and the social fabric of many communities and the schools that serve them. These changes compound the more enduring economic challenges long faced by many people living in "abandoned" inner cities and rural communities, as well as those people living on Native American reservations.

During the same period, waves of immigrants and refugees in search of a safer, more stable and economically productive life have moved to virtually all corners of the nation. Traveling to the United States in hopes of a better life for their children and themselves, these newcomers often arrive with few material resources and speaking a language other than English. Many come from generations of poverty in their previous countries, and many are victims of famine and war. They often join the millions of other U.S. adults, adolescents, and children living in poverty.

For many educators, this reality means witnessing an increase in the number of students who live in poverty and perhaps the number who are learning English as their second, third, or fourth language. Some of those increases may be among children and youth from families who come from generational poverty; others may be from working-class families barely surviving under the strain of falling further and further behind or middle-class families angry and afraid because the security they once felt and the choices they once had are no longer available to them.

Educators are more important to this country than ever (although that is not likely to be the headline in tomorrow's newspaper, news alert, or blog post). The quality of education that individuals are afforded and the level of education they attain are arguably more tightly linked to their life outcomes than ever before. To not earn a high school diploma severely compromises their life chances, and a diploma is not enough. As Celia, a Latina elementary school teacher, told us,

> I have a sense of urgency because I realize that I had to bury a lot of friends. I went to a lot of funerals in high school. A lot of bad stuff happened, and I also saw that those who went to school like myself or other students who were lucky enough to get out and go to college, they're still around. They're happily married. They have homes. They have careers, just like I do. The only difference was, we got an education.

In the next chapters we focus on what educators can do to disrupt poverty in their sphere of influence. We describe five poverty-disrupting actions: building caring relationships and advocacy (Chapter 3); holding high expectations and providing needed support (Chapter 4); committing to equity (Chapter 5); assuming professional accountability for learning (Chapter 6); and marshaling the courage and will to take action (Chapter 7).

 ## APPLYING YOUR LEARNING TO YOUR PRACTICE

Autobiographical Sketch

Write a one-to-two-page autobiographical sketch about the socioeconomic class in which you grew up. What are the factors with which you identify in that class? With what socioeconomic class do you currently identify? How do these class-based identities influence your professional practice?

Application of Learning Matrix

To help you apply what you are learning to your professional practice, see Appendix A. Each chapter's high-leverage question is listed there, with space to list each student and reflect on what you know. Teachers with more than 25 students may want to use multiple matrices or select a particular class period. For this chapter, here is the high-leverage question: What do I know about each of my student's living conditions?

Challenging Our Mental Maps:
Learning, Unlearning, and Relearning Summary Table

Pause for a few minutes and use the following questions to consider your current thinking as it relates to the information and ideas presented in this chapter.

Learning: What conceptions did you hold about poverty before reading this chapter?

Unlearning: How, if at all, did the chapter challenge your beliefs or thinking?

Relearning: How might this "challenge to your thinking" or new idea be beneficial or helpful to you?

Action: What *action* will you take, and why?

As you consider your answers and progress through this book, record your answers for each chapter in the summary table supplied in Appendix B. The summary table provides you with a model for exploring your mental map, reflecting on current practice, developing your theory of action, and planning next steps.

 COMMUNITIES OF PRACTICE:
Extending Your Learning with Others

- Share with each other the ways in which the information in the chapter challenged your mental map of poverty and people in poverty.
- Provide and discuss examples of how gaining an accurate understanding of poverty has actually affected a student and his or her achievement and success in school.

- What questions does this chapter raise related to your classroom, school, and district?
- How well do we understand the adverse poverty-related influences on our students?
- In what *systematic* ways do we share our knowledge of how these factors affect our students? Think of a student or group of students as an example and discuss how you know this information and what you are doing about it.
- How can the information about welfare help us better serve our students, and what questions does it raise?
- How are students stereotyped in our school? What are some examples?

VOICES FROM POVERTY

CONNIE

In 1992, both of my boys were killed in a car accident. It was a single-car accident; my son was driving. There were four kids in the car. Everybody was killed.

At that time, I was a school bus driver and I desperately wanted to work with kids because my parenting had been cut short. The empty-nest syndrome kicked in, big time. The kids I drove for were in poverty—Section Eight housing. I knew that I needed these kids. After a couple more years, I transferred into assistant teaching at the high school level. Bottom line: I needed to do something other than bus driving. I wanted to be around kids more.

I was in love with teaching. I needed to be with children, and I knew that I had something that I could give. At that point, I started college and worked as a teacher's aide for a time. I now have a master's-plus, and I've worked in three very high-poverty areas. I've been teaching about 13 years.

My mom had a 3rd grade education. She was a daughter of a drunk, who was also a sharecropper. My dad was a union carpenter, so we moved a lot. By the time I was in 7th grade, we had moved nine times between five states in the South.

In the middle of my 7th grade year, we moved out west to a piece of land in the middle of a desert in a trailer that had no electricity and no water. I didn't realize that we were in poverty until we got there. The itty-bitty, podunk school was a pretty good school, but they didn't know that we didn't have electricity. I did my homework by a kerosene lamp, and we hauled water to take a bath. Five gallons at night. You could take baths, flush the toilet, brush your teeth, wash your hair, whatever you got to do; but five gallons is what you got.

It seemed like my parents were always chasing from one rainbow dream to another rainbow dream. Every time we packed up to go, we had to forfeit something. We never really had Christmas, but the best Christmas I remember was spent in that trailer without the electricity or the water. My little brother and I went out in the desert, and we got us a Charlie Brown Christmas tree. It was nothing more than a creosote bush, and we brought it back to the house and we decorated it with crayons, colored stuff.

My brother, who's older than me by about six years, molested me when I was 7. I had an uncle that was all touchy-feely. When you're dealing with high poverty, you deal with overcrowding; and when you deal with overcrowding, you're sometimes going to deal with incest, you're going to deal with overeating, you're going to deal with the emotional traumas. Those are things that can come along with poverty. I not only experienced it, but have seen it too many times.

I got pregnant in high school. My husband is not the biological father of my children. The biological father and I divorced when my youngest one was about 3 years old. It turned out that he didn't like to keep a job, so I lived in poverty with my kids.

We lived without electricity a lot of times. We lived in homes that were condemned. Finally, one day I just said, "You know what? If my kids are going to go without food, then we can starve to death without him too."

I went back to a town where I knew they were building an addition to a steel mill. I went to work as a carpenter. That's where I met my husband and my boys' adopted dad, in 1980. We moved north in 1988.

When the boys were in school, we decided that we would try to be substitutes at the local schools. They trained us to be bus drivers, so we would drive a bus in the morning, work a part-time job in the middle of the day, and then drive a bus in the afternoon. That's what we did until the boys died. Then things changed quite a bit.

So now I'm a SPED teacher. And I love my job. My kids are a hoot. They make me laugh. They are a blast to be with. I get paid to play. ■

3 DISRUPTION 1: BUILDING CARING RELATIONSHIPS AND ADVOCATING FOR STUDENTS

I am on morning duty. I watch Tia run behind a tree, button up her jacket, and it's 90 degrees already. I talk to the other on-duty teacher, excuse myself, and walk over to Tia. As I'm approaching, I quickly realize she's wearing exactly the same thing she was wearing in class yesterday. OK, I get why she has bundled up with her jacket, trying to make it not look like she's wearing the same thing. "Hi, honey," I say to her. "Let's go to our room and get you some clothes for today. You can pick something out, wear it, and then when you're done with it, put it in the box. I'll wash it and bring it back tomorrow." Her little face lights up with a smile. Tia comes from a difficult situation, but when she gets to school, she really tries. She knows we're here for her.

—*Alva, 2nd Grade Teacher*

 ANSWERING THE "WHO" QUESTION: A 100-Word Reflection

What are the images, assumptions, and stories you carry in your mind (your mental map) about why *people live in poverty?* _____

_____

_____

_____

_____

ANSWERING THE "WHAT" QUESTION:
What the Research Tells Us

Developing Relationships: Your First, Best Strategy

James, one of the teachers we interviewed, was on to something when he said the following:

> Some teachers struggle with students in poverty because they don't understand.... They miss the point. Teaching is about relationships. Learning will not occur without applying it to the core of the individual. Learning is superficial without the element of the student-teacher bond.

According to Sam Redding (2013), senior learning specialist for the Center on Innovations in Learning, "Classroom culture... emanates from the personal relationships of the teacher with her students and the relationship among the students... through the student's eyes, the teacher, by virtue of her role, is worthy of respect. By her actions she adds to or subtracts from that appraisal" (p. 8).

Building caring and trusting relationships between you and your students and among the students is your first, most powerful strategy for successfully teaching any student, but especially those who live in poverty. When we interviewed Melissa, a 20-year veteran teacher who grew up in poverty, she told us the following:

> Honestly, I see all of my kids growing in different ways, from their academics to their personality to the way they interact with one another. The biggest thing that I feel has helped me is making sure that my kids feel comfortable with me and that they're comfortable with each other. On a daily basis, I always tell them I love them, and I mean it because I feel like they are a part of me. I see them every day; if anything, I spend so much more time with them than anybody else. And in these two years that we've spent together, I feel like they know me so well and I know them so well, and I feel like that's definitely contributed to our daily success in learning.

The nature of the student-teacher relationship is fundamental to everything else that happens in our classrooms. Relationships characterized by mutual respect and trust increase student effort and motivation (Quaglia, Fox, & Corso, 2010; Redding, 2013); build resilience (Johnson, 2008; Stride

& Cutcher, 2015); and improve academic achievement (Bryk & Schneider, 2002; Hattie, 2009).

Increased Effort and Motivation

Student-teacher relationships correlate with increased motivation and effort. With a sample size of more than 500,000 student surveys, Russ Quaglia and his colleagues from the Quaglia Institute can be confident in their finding that building caring relationships with students increases student effort and motivation.

> Students who said they put forth their best effort were twice as likely as students who said they did not to agree with the statement, "Teachers care about me as an individual." Similarly, students who said they put forth their best effort were twice as likely to agree that "Teachers respect students." (Quaglia, Fox, & Corso, 2010)

Effort, more than innate ability, is important for succeeding academically (Dweck, 2006). Students are motivated and will put forth effort for teachers whom they view as dedicated to their academic success (Redding, 2013).

Increased Resilience and Risk Taking

Resilience and risk taking are also critical to learning, and ample evidence shows that caring relationships with adults (including educators) provide a protective factor that builds resilience in students (Benard, 1997; Johnson, 2008; Stride & Cutcher, 2015). Although teachers, particularly those in high-poverty schools, can sometimes feel as though broader forces outside of their control make the impact they can have questionable, in an eight-year study, Bruce Johnson (2008) found students were motivated to take risks when they viewed their teachers as interrupting the *everyday experiences* that threaten their well-being. Moreover, this outcome did not require heroic efforts; rather, it was "the little things" teachers do that made the difference (p. 390). Knowing students well, being interested in their lives, valuing them as people, and "just being there" gave students a sense of well-being and increased their coping strategies (p. 391). Other researchers found that engaging students in creative endeavors places teachers in the position of helping students to value their uniqueness, "overcome their need to be 'right,'" and understand failure as a natural part of learning, all of which builds resilience and greater willingness to take risks (Stride & Cutcher, 2015, p. 12).

Improved Academic Achievement

Anthony Bryk and Barbara Schneider (2002) conducted a nearly decade-long study of 400 Chicago public schools to explore the relationship between student achievement and relational trust. They defined relational trust as a combination of four factors: (1) mutual respect, (2) personal regard, (3) competence in core responsibilities, and (4) personal integrity. They compared academic productivity over time with the level of relational trust in each school and came to this conclusion: one in two schools with high levels of trust had improved academic productivity, whereas only one in seven schools with low levels of relational trust demonstrated improved academic productivity. Relational trust matters profoundly.

John Hattie (2009) also found a strong correlation between student-teacher relationships and student achievement. Classes led by teachers whose professional practice was "person centered" demonstrated greater engagement, more respect of self and others, fewer behavior problems, more student-directed and student-regulated strategies, and higher student achievement (p. 119).

Jon, who has been teaching at the middle-school level for 15 years, builds relationships with his students in myriad ways. For example, he makes a set of cards—similar to baseball cards—on which he keeps "stats" about each of his students. He notes their likes and dislikes, their interests, and their hopes and dreams. He also sends home postcards with positive comments about each student on a regular basis, and keeps a spreadsheet of his interactions with students to ensure he is not leaving the "quiet kids" out. Jon understands the link between the student-teacher relationship and student achievement. He told us,

> a lot of these kids who get a Below Basic score before I have them, and then they score Advanced on their [state achievement test], I want to say that their teachers actually taught them very well, but these students didn't want to perform for them when it came down to the actual test day.... But when you're encouraging them and you're loving on them and you build that relationship all year, when it comes time for the test, they kind of want to pull through for you. I think that's what it came down to.

Teachers as Models, Mentors, Interveners, and Extended Family

Students living in poverty benefit in a variety of ways from a caring relationship with their teacher. Teachers can serve as role models and mentors who help students break the cycle of poverty and "intervene" in ways that foster resilience, including assuming roles that are family-like in nature.

Teachers as Models

When students truly trust their teachers and view them as people who care about them, they care about their teachers in return. Such relational trust can be the basis for teachers to effectively model learning behaviors for students. When students see their teachers taking risks, reading to learn something new, expressing themselves in writing, and so on, they will voluntarily "try out some of those behaviors as well" (Haberman, 1996, p. 56).

Although modeling may be how teachers encourage students to engage, teachers eventually help shift students' reasons for engaging from the extrinsic reward of a caring relationship to the intrinsic rewards of learning something new and gaining self-confidence and a sense of efficacy (Haberman, 1996). Anton, a high school English teacher who teaches primarily refugee students, said he spends the first part of each semester "frontloading a work ethic." As he explained, he models a willingness to meet students where they are academically, scaffolding their learning in a variety of ways, including spending a significant amount of one-on-one time with them outside of the school day, particularly at the beginning of the school year. He does this, in part, to help them see the value of effort. He says this approach nearly always pays off, with students adopting a willingness to persevere—a habit, they tell him, that extends into other areas of their lives.

Teachers as Mentors

Teachers are often in the best position to show students how education can benefit them. Too often students who live in poverty, especially those in generational poverty, have not known anyone for whom education has "worked" to improve their lives. "For people in poverty to learn new information, new ways of thinking and behaving, they need identification with someone who is making it. Someone who is practicing the new behavior and providing encouragement that they also can do it…" (Beegle, 2007, p. 89).

When teachers are mentors, they are bearers of hope. You may have heard the expression, "Hope is not a strategy." We are not sure who originated that perspective, but we fear it conveys a notion that hope is not valuable. Quite the contrary, hope is invaluable. For students experiencing the chaos and trauma poverty can inflict, providing a guiding light can give them the hope they need to persist. As elementary teacher Anna advised, "Give kids hope, help them see their future." Poverty-disrupting teachers know mentoring can have a profoundly positive effect on students who live in poverty.

Teachers as Interveners

In his study of "at risk" youth, Bruce Johnson (2008) found "intervening" on students' behalf was one of seven teacher actions that provided protective factors and engendered resilience. Surprisingly, it was the "ordinariness" of the teachers' actions and attitudes that was important because they are "within the capacity of most classroom teachers to implement" (p. 390). This finding was also true for the teachers we interviewed. It was the everyday things, within their sphere of influence, that made a difference in their students' lives. They described multiple ways in which they intervened to ensure students' well-being—from providing for basic needs such as a snack or mittens to ensuring students had everything they needed to complete their homework. The small things mattered. As chemistry teacher Lizzy explained, "Dry skin is a big deal for African Americans. I know that having lotion is important to me, so I make sure my students know I keep some in the closet for their use." David, who had been an elementary teacher, described the influence of everyday interactions with Todd, one of his students:

> Life had been a struggle for Todd. His stepfather had physically abused him. He was quiet and shy. He did not want to participate in class, but when he did, he was so smart. He just needed encouragement… I was one of the only males in the school. I became kind of that surrogate father figure to a lot of the kids, Todd being one of them. I just encouraged him academically. We worked together after school. I would deliberately have things for him to do

before school, so he would come in early in the morning and hang out with me and help me. I just really built him up, built his self-esteem, and got him to recognize that what happened wasn't his fault and didn't need to guide his future.

Teachers as Extended Family

Scholars in New Zealand who have spent more than a decade theorizing and studying attributes of teachers who succeed with Maori children, many of whom live in poverty, conclude that the nature of the student-teacher relationship is a key factor affecting their educational achievement (Bishop, 2008; Bishop & Berryman, 2006; Bishop, Berryman, Cavanagh, & Teddy, 2007). Teachers who created an extended family-like atmosphere in their classrooms were successful in motivating, engaging, and empowering their students, as well as improving their academic achievement. An extended family-like relationship in Maori culture, known as *whanaungatanga* (far-know-na-tounge-ah), is characterized as "warm interpersonal interactions, group solidarity, shared responsibility for one another, cheerful cooperation for group ends, and corporate responsibility for group property, material or nonmaterial (e.g., knowledge)..." (Bishop, Ladwig, & Berryman, 2014, p. 189).

Caring Student-Teacher Relationships: The Foundation of a Poverty-Disrupting Classroom Culture

Student-teacher relationships serve as the foundation for each of the other attributes of a classroom culture that disrupts poverty. These relationships are formed through daily interactions, each with the power to influence the relationship positively or negatively. Success with students who live in poverty depends upon a theory of action that privileges relationships over all other aspects of teaching, and an understanding that relationship building must be the paramount consideration if learning is to occur. As high school teacher Lizzy explained,

> You can be as smart as a whip in regard to your content knowledge. You can deliver instruction in a certain manner, but if you don't have the relationship that you need with your students, they won't necessarily receive your

message. And so, if you start with that relationship piece, everything else will follow in line.

Enlisting students as coconstructors of knowledge, engaging them in dialogue as opposed to one-way questioning, providing them with timely feedback, providing opportunities to self-direct at least some of their learning activities, and ensuring the chance to learn in teams are constructivist approaches shown to be effective with students who live in poverty (Knapp & Adelman, 1995). However, use of constructivist strategies is unlikely to happen in classrooms where teachers do not foster a sense of family between themselves and students and among students. Conversely, in classrooms with an extended family-like classroom culture, the use of these approaches increases exponentially (Bishop, Ladwig, & Berryman, 2014). This reality reminds us of the importance of connecting the "who" and the "why" questions to the "what" and the "how." Our beliefs about students who live in poverty influence how we relate to them; our expectations for them (see Chapter 4); our willingness to level the playing field (see Chapter 5); our sense of responsibility for student learning (see Chapter 6); and our inclination to challenge inequity, and if needed, the status quo (see Chapter 7).

Poverty-disrupting teachers are able to see through poverty to the *person*. They know themselves, they know their students, and they understand the adverse effects poverty can have on lives and learning. In her book *See Poverty... Be the Difference*, Donna Beegle (2007), drawing on the work of Knapp (1984), explains that to build enough mutual trust in a relationship to accomplish specific outcomes (such as student learning), we must eventually "suspend judgment" and "see" others as being like us—possessing both strengths and weaknesses—and assume they are making the best choices given the "traumatic conditions" they often live in (p. 96).

Questioning our assumptions enables us to adopt a resilience perspective, rather than the predominantly held deficit view of students living in poverty. It also focuses us on the assets that students who live in poverty bring to the table, which "might just be the most essential ingredient in the effective relationship recipe..." (Gorski, 2013, p. 134). Additionally, teachers who reject deficit ideology have been found to be happier in their job (Robinson, 2007, in Gorski, 2013).

ANSWERING THE "HOW" QUESTION:
Tips from Teachers

Nine Practical Suggestions for Building Relationships

Ideas for building relationships with students abound. Social media has greatly enhanced our ability to share practical strategies and good ideas with each other. The teachers we interviewed had much wisdom to impart about building relationships with their students, but the most important aspect of the advice they offered was to be intentional—to explicitly plan for relationship building, just as you plan for instruction. We have synthesized their advice into nine strategies and tips to support your efforts to build relationships.

1. Begin with Four Critical Building Blocks

Identification, authenticity, empathy, and trust are four important building blocks for establishing and maintaining relationships with students.

Identification. To identify with another person is to find common ground. As we began our interview with David, an elementary school teacher, he told us he'd never grown past 5th grade humor, and for this reason he could "really form a bond" with his students. He explained,

> I tell the student teachers [I supervise in my classroom] to go home, turn on the shows they would normally pass by to be able to relate to what students are watching and talking about. If students place an emphasis on something and a value on it, shouldn't I [as the teacher] know about it? This is a great way to build a relationship with students.

Authenticity. Teachers spoke not only of getting to know students, but also of the importance of allowing themselves to be known by students. Every teacher mentioned the value of authenticity—of being themselves. Leslie, who had been teaching for 10 years, claimed,

> Opening up to [students] about my struggles and my life builds that student-teacher relationship ... Let students see your flaws. Be human. [It helps students] understand to be accepting of that in everyone.

Celia echoed Leslie's advice, asserting, "Being authentic is critical to building student-teacher relationships. Share real stories about your life. Let students see you on a personal level."

Empathy. Empathy plays a critical role in developing caring relationships with students (Johnson, 2008; Noddings, 2010). Many teachers discussed the importance of understanding the difference between sympathy and empathy. *Sympathy* was viewed as feeling sorry for students and lowering standards out of a false belief that students living in poverty could not meet high standards. *Empathy,* on the other hand, was having an awareness of the students' challenging life circumstances while maintaining high standards and providing the support needed to meet those standards. Celia talked about the importance of understanding students' fears, and Anna professed,

> I am just flat-out honest with students. [I tell them] I care about you. I care about what they are going through; if they have things going on in their lives they want to talk about, I will make time for students and let them know that.

Likewise, Jon explained that he tells his students, "I can only imagine what it would be like if I had that kind of struggle. That's a lot for you to take on." He continued,

> Usually, before I say that, there's very little eye contact, but whenever I give little expressions like that to identify with them, to empathize with them, all of a sudden, their body language changes. They're no longer shrugging their shoulders when I ask them a question. They're making eye contact with me, and I'm finally able to break through a barrier that was up and connect with them and then take it to the next step to be successful with them. Without empathy, without reaching the kid and proving to the kid that you really care, you might as well have them watch a video. What good are we as human beings if we can't empathize?

Connie addressed empathy a bit more directly:

> Anyone teaching kids who live in poverty needs to be empathetic, not sympathetic. There's a big difference. People in poverty don't need your sympathy; that's the last thing they need. They need to know how to fish; they don't need somebody to give them a stinking fish!

Trust. Developing trust is a critical aspect of fostering relationships with students and among students. As Leslie asserted, "Students need to trust teachers, need to let them in. They need to feel comfortable [to do so]." Breeding relational trust requires mutual respect between student and teacher; teachers need to demonstrate personal regard for students, and students learn it is safe to take risks when teachers model integrity (Bryk & Schneider, 2002). In thinking back on one of his most vulnerable students, Jon explained how he developed trust between him and the student:

> I was consistent in my approach with him, which was calm, never sarcastic. I wouldn't argue with him. I'd let him know the expectations. I would genuinely listen to him. I genuinely wanted to hear how he felt, why he felt that way, and then we'd explore different ways [for him] to try to express himself that were appropriate.

Jon told us he has three rules for building relationships with students: (1) take nothing personally (and don't take myself so seriously), (2) always converse with the student but never argue, and (3) always be genuine (never use sarcasm).

2. View Parents/Families/Caregivers as a Key Resource

Several teachers described how they developed relationships with parents, families, and caregivers. These teachers were intentional about getting to know families in order to gain a better understanding of their students and to gain an authentic partner. It was not unusual for them to conduct home visits or attend events of religious or cultural importance to the families. Miranda told us she "builds relationships with parents and families" in part because she "values the insight they have into their child," and Leslie explained the reason she works hard to establish such relationships, saying, "There is a big difference in how hard [students] work if they know that there is home and school communication. They'll work harder sometimes for parents than they normally do if they know I'm checking in on them. So, I think it's important we're all on the same page."

Connie knows the parents of her high school students care deeply about their kids and their futures, and she regularly connects with her students' parents. She knows a good relationship with parents is essential.

To develop a good relationship with your kids, call their parents and tell them something good that that kid has done. You catch them being good and share that with the parents. If that kid has done 25 things wrong, you find those 2 things that you'll die on a hill for, and the rest of it you let go. Share a couple of good things you found with the parents *and* the kid! You can't gain either of their respect until you've given it to them. You have to give it first. I've heard colleagues talk about, "They've got to give me some respect because I'm the teacher." Actually, you're the older person, and the situation needs a hero. So be the hero.

3. Sweat the Small Stuff:
Everyday Interactions Make the Difference

It does not take herculean effort to foster relationships with students. Studies have demonstrated that students believe teachers are "good" teachers when they attend to the everyday interactions they have with them (Dryden, Johnson, Howard, & McGuire, 1998). For example, listening to students, treating them with respect, taking the time to ask about their lives, and telling them about your life make a big difference. With his students, David does something he calls the "two-minute drill." He explained, "I do the two-minute drill with each student, one per day. Go for a walk and ask them questions about their lives, aspirations, favorite video games, what they do when they get home, etc." He tracks whom he has talked to and whom he has not, to ensure he gets to every student.

For Jon, greeting every student is important. Most of his greetings are standard "meet students at the door and ask how they are" types of greetings, but he also develops personal, "secret" handshakes with individual students that rival a complex choreographed dance routine. Amazingly, he remembers them all, and so do his students—even years after they leave his classroom and the school.

4. Be Fully Present, Listen, and Set Aside Time to Bond

Several teachers described needing to "be there" for students. They described "bonding time," which they orchestrated in the form of lunch or before- or after-school time with students, in some cases on a rotating basis. They stressed the importance of letting the student lead the conversation. Additionally, teachers were frank about the challenge of taking the time to "be present." Here's how Nina described her own situation:

I would find myself obsessing about plans and preparation for the upcoming period, or even ruminating on what had occurred in the prior class. The "busyness" of teaching does not lend itself well to the idea of being in the present. Ironically, the days I was most tired and found that I only had the energy to deal with the things that were immediately in front of me were also the days I connected more with kids. I am not suggesting that sleep deprivation is the answer, of course, but rather that we try to continuously bring our thoughts back to what is immediately in front of us, and invest ourselves in the lives of our kids through those present moments. The seemingly unnecessary dialogue and informal discussions take on a different meaning when we are fully present with our students, and those moments might also be the ones that produce genuine connections.

For Connie, it's all about listening:

Listening. Being willing to listen. Kids are hungry for somebody to listen to what they've got to say. When you listen, they will talk to you, they will tell you things. They will tell you their fears. As soon as you start listening, you gain their respect. Listening is the best thing you can do for them, because too many people in their lives aren't.

5. Teach Routines and Provide Structures

Nearly every teacher mentioned the importance of establishing, teaching, and practicing classroom routines as a way of ensuring a predictable and productive learning environment. In the first week of the semester, Lizzy establishes such routines through a series of nonacademic team-building tasks. She explained her theory of action:

[T]o ensure students get accustomed to working together, being dependent upon one another when they need to, trusting each other, I begin the semester with team building. These tasks are in line with what I'm looking for them to do in the classroom.... I do a lot of collaborating, cooperative groups, things of that nature where you have to be willing to group with anybody. I tell them, "When I group you with anyone in the room, it is a life lesson, because in the real world you don't know who you're going to be working with. It may not be your best friend, but you still should be able to [work with them]." [T]hey're not necessarily accustomed to working with one another. And so, all of those things come together during that one-week period where we just have a great time with each other but realize we can trust each other as well. All of that is a part of that relationship building that I think is key to them just receiving anything that I give. And so the state testing just comes right along with that.

Marissa, who loops with her students, teaching them for both 1st and 2nd grade, described how establishing routines and structures early on leads to empowerment of children and ownership in the way "things are done" in their classroom.

> The first day they're like little ducklings. They follow you everywhere, and they need constant reminders. And now on a daily basis they surprise me. They can run a lot of the things on their own. They are so amazing at it, and they remind each other about their daily expectations... I feel like we've definitely built that relationship with one another.

Many teachers noted the need to establish specific routines and structures for individual students. For example, one of Leslie's students who lived in an unpredictable, stress-filled environment struggled with anxiety that was at times debilitating. Leslie discovered if she gave him a meaningful job to do, such as taking something to the office, watering the classroom plants, or organizing something for her, he would feel "useful and needed," which in turn calmed him so that he was able to productively rejoin the class.

6. Create a Sense of Extended Family and Community

Nearly every teacher we interviewed mentioned developing family-like relationships and a cooperative community as being critically important to creating a safe learning environment for all students. Through her investment of time and planning, Lizzy said her classes became "somewhat of a family just based upon the team-building activities [in which she joins her students] and getting to know one another, trusting one another in ways that we've never done before."

As a 5th grade teacher, David chose Harry Potter as a theme to create community. After all, his students are Harry's age when the series begins. He said, "Students feel like they belong to something bigger," guided by the class motto: "We rise and fall together." He went on to explain how that worked.

There were two students who were horrible to each other. Instead of separating them, I put them together, let them know they would share this room an entire year, and that because we rise and fall together, they needed to figure out how to make it work and by the end of the year they would be comrades; and they were.

Miranda, who teaches 1st grade, described the ethos she works to create among her students:

Working together in groups, I feel like a lot of these students know each other really well; they know about each other's strengths and weaknesses, and it's not something that's talked about; it's never pointed out. When they see that other students make the achievement in something that they're working on, I do not even have to let the class know anything. They just start cheering that student on automatically. I feel like promoting group-work cooperation is another strategy to constantly get them to get to know one another.

7. Move Beyond Defined Roles

Most teachers we interviewed pointed to moving beyond their "job description" as key to their success in developing relationships with students and families. For instance, Celia talked about the significance of "attending soccer games, birthday parties, and being available after school hours," and Anna advised, "Show students you care about them as a person. Go to their sporting events, baptisms, etc. Identify with their lives."

8. Harness the Power of Creativity

Engaging students in creative enterprises, which move them out of logical thinking for a time, provides opportunities for teachers to nurture students' individuality and helps students value their uniqueness. Creative endeavors also encourage risk taking and a view of failure as a natural part of the creative process. Such experiences support students to move away from the fear that they must find one (right) answer, builds resilience (Stride & Cutcher, 2015), and provides another lens through which to "see" students.

9. Build a Network of Support for Your Students and Yourself

Enlisting support for yourself and your students, several teachers told us, was a vital step in building strong relationships. Miranda spoke of the imperative for fostering social capital among families as a source of support for students and herself. She not only was a leader among her colleagues in finding creative ways to get parents and families together schoolwide, but also held her own "parent/family" functions.

Not long after he began teaching, David realized the critical role played by all the adults in a school. He described partnerships he formed with kitchen staff, custodians, and school secretaries to garner resources or establish mentorships for students. Celia and Jon each had collegial relationships with people they called their "accountability partners"—other educators they met with regularly. In each case, the partners established individual goals for the year and then held each other accountable for working toward those goals.

The nine strategies presented here provide the building blocks of strong classroom relationships. In addition, the teachers we interviewed described specific activities they use to build relationship with and among students. Figure 3.1 provides a list of these activities.

 APPLYING YOUR LEARNING TO YOUR PRACTICE

- What feelings surface when you think about students who live in poverty? How about their parents? Are the feelings different?
- What do you believe most "gets in your way" as you build relationships with students who live in poverty?
- Think of a time when a student who lived in poverty surprised you. What happened? Why were you surprised?
- Think of someone who has been a model or mentor for you. What made the relationship work? What did this person do to influence your thinking and actions?

FIGURE 3.1 | Ideas for Building Relationships

Sit Down/Stand Up Activity—Make statements and ask students to stand up or sit down in response; for example, "Sit down if you are an older brother," "Stand up if you are the youngest." With older students, gather information related to students' interests, aspirations, learning preferences, or problem solving through surveys, inventories, and interviews.

Two-Minute Drill—Conduct a two-minute drill with each student, one per day. Go for a walk and ask them questions about their lives, aspirations, favorite video games, and what they do when they get home.

A Little Bag About Me—Ask students to put three small things in a bag that can be used to tell others something about themselves. Older students can be asked to create an artifact that represents something important to them.

Apple Glyphs—Students create a picture or collage about themselves, cut it into pieces, and exchange it with a classmate.

Stacking Cups—Using only certain parts of their bodies or restricting the use of certain parts (like no hands), have students work in teams and depend on each other to make the highest stack of cups.

Desert Island—Ask students to pretend they are stranded on an island and can have only a certain number of items. They individually select an item they believe would be important and explain to each other why they selected it. After discussing what each of the items can be used for, they have one more opportunity to change their minds, but in the end, they all have to agree.

Baseball Cards—Make a set of cards (like baseball cards) complete with statistics about your students—contact information, likes and dislikes, interests, and aspirations.

The Name Game—Make a deal with students that no homework will be assigned until you can recite each student's name as he or she leaves the room.

Tech to Connect—Use Edmodo, Facebook, or similar applications to create a virtual space for learning about each other and connecting with families.

Check-In—Be intentional about checking in with a few students each day and keep reminders to follow up. Track your "check-ins" and be sure to get to every student.

Dialogue Journals—Journal back and forth with each student. Begin by telling them they can ask questions about you and you will respond as you begin to know each other. These journals can be a very powerful strategy for getting to know students. Students will often share information about themselves in writing that they would not otherwise share.

Parent/Family Outreach—Gather phone numbers and e-mail addresses and reach out frequently to share positive news.

Humans of [Insert Your School's Name]—As a spin-off of Humans of New York (http://www.humansofnewyork.com/), allow students to create videos as a way to get to know each other's stories.

Scar Memoirs—Writing a "scar memoir" is an opportunity for students to reflect on a critical event in their life and make it meaningful. It invites them to explore their lives, tapping into an experience and observing it through their writing in order to mine it for self-discovery, to learn a lesson, or simply to "get something off their chest."

Notice Three Things—Students feel valued when they are "seen." Notice at least three things about each student (suspending judgment) throughout the year.

Bell Ringers or Warm-Ups—Start every class by asking one or two students to relate something about themselves, a recent event, or current topic of interest. Rotate through every student.

Secret Handshakes—Create, practice, and memorize secret handshakes with your students, with secret meanings behind the movements.

Application of Learning Matrix

To help you apply what you are learning to your professional practice, see Appendix A. Each chapter's high-leverage question is listed there, with space to list each student and reflect on what you know. Teachers with more than 25 students may want to use multiple matrices or select a particular class period. For this chapter, here is the high-leverage question: What assets, strengths, or cultural fund of knowledge does _____ [student's name] bring to the classroom?

Challenging Our Mental Maps:
Learning, Unlearning, and Relearning Summary

Pause for a few minutes and use the following questions to consider your current thinking as it relates to the information and ideas presented in this chapter.

Learning: What conceptions did you hold about teacher-student relationships before reading this chapter?

Unlearning: How, if at all, did the chapter challenge your beliefs or thinking?

Relearning: How might this "challenge to your thinking" or new idea be beneficial or helpful to you?

Action: What *action* will you take, and why?

As you consider your answers and progress through this book, record your answers for each chapter in the summary table supplied in Appendix B. The summary table provides you with a model for exploring your mental map, reflecting on current practice, developing your theory of action, and planning next steps.

 ## COMMUNITIES OF PRACTICE:
Extending Your Learning with Others

- How do we intentionally build relationships in our school? Are those efforts enough? If not, what else needs to be done?
- How well do we know our students? What did we learn by using the Application of Learning Matrix?

- What are some examples of a relationship with a student that prompted improvement in performance or attitude? What can we learn from these bright spots?
- Do our students trust us? How do we know?
- How might we further enhance our trust in each other?
- What classroom practices are teachers and other educators successfully using to foster relationships among the students?

Challenging Stereotypes to Build Caring Relationships

Stereotype 1: People live in poverty because of individual deficiencies such as "poor" moral character or "poor" choices.

This stereotype is quite common, and left unexamined is likely to pose a barrier to the development of positive, productive relationships with your students and their families who live in poverty. Studies have demonstrated that 9 out of 10 people believe poverty is caused by individual choices (Wilson, 2009, as cited in Ullucci & Howard, 2015). Although some individuals are, indeed, in poverty because of their personal choices, these instances do not explain poverty's existence on a wider scale—mass impoverishment (Ullucci & Howard, 2015). As we discussed in Chapter 2, African Americans and Latinos disproportionally live in poverty, as do women and households headed by single women. To attribute "poor choices" or "poor moral character" to an entire group of people at best has questionable face validity and at worst is racist or sexist. Also, poverty is more concentrated and persistent in certain regions of the United States, including tribal lands, the South, abandoned inner cities, and rural communities. Justifying poverty as the result of individual deficits or personal choices makes little common sense when examining poverty's geographical and historical distribution trends. Reasons for poverty's existence are much more multifaceted, as Paul Gorski (2012) notes:

> To believe, for example, that poor people are poor solely because of their own deficiencies, [we] must ignore a slew of sociopolitical realities related to poverty and class, including inequitable access to schooling and scarcity of living wage jobs. (p. 307)

A small logging and mining community, Kathleen's home town provides a good example of some of the systemic factors that have led to increased poverty in many rural communities whose economic base has historically been dependent upon industries consisting of natural-resource extraction, like logging, mining, and fishing. Advances in technology, environmental policy, international trade policy, and disempowerment of unions have all taken their toll on the economic and social fabric of such places. This is only one example of systemic dynamics resulting in increases in poverty. In his book *Urban Injustice: How Ghettos Happen,* David Hilfiker (2002) asserts,

> [T]he primary causes of poverty lie not in individual behavior at all, but in opposite social and historical structures, in forces outside of any single person's control… the essential causes of American poverty lie elsewhere: in the paucity of jobs on which someone might support a family, in inadequate access to health care and child care, in meager educational resources, in specific governmental policies, in nonexistent vocational training, in the workings of the criminal justice system… in a painful history of slavery, segregation, and discrimination. (p. xii)

Attributing poverty to deficiencies in individuals rather than inequities in opportunity has increasingly emerged in popular thinking since the mid-1970s. Before that time, studies had consistently shown Americans pointed to systemic considerations, such as those we discussed in detail in Chapter 2 (Gorski, 2012). Several converging factors contributed to this shift. A growing endorsement of the "culture of poverty" theory (see Chapter 2), scholars have argued, was used to justify a change in government expenditures away from those in poverty to those higher on the economic ladder (mainly through the tax code). Painting a picture of those in poverty as being responsible for their situation made it more palpable to justify a change in government spending priorities. Paul Gorski (2012) explains:

> During his failed bid for the 1976 Republican presidential primary endorsement, [Ronald] Reagan often repeated the story of Linda Taylor, a woman from the south side of Chicago who defrauded the government out of roughly $8,000.00 in welfare claims by using four aliases. Reagan exaggerated considerably during his speeches, suggesting that Taylor, who he called a *"welfare queen,"* had collected more than $150,000 and used more than 80 aliases, a mischaracterization uncovered at the time by the *Washington Star* . . . . (p. 306)

Journalists and others have concluded that Reagan's "welfare queen" did not exist—she was created by Reagan speechwriters (Gorski, 2012). This depiction of people living in poverty and the term *welfare queen* left "an indelible mark" on popular opinion in the United States and "established it, with all of its stereotypic insinuations, firmly in the U.S. lexicon, where it has remained for more than 30 years . . ." (Gorski, 2012, p. 306).

Stereotyping people in poverty has consequences for our students and ourselves. Even if stereotypes are held only tacitly, students' sense that they are being stereotyped can negatively affect their learning and emotional well-being (Steele & Aronson, 1995). Too often stereotypes are used to justify achievement gaps, when the real problem is the gap between students in poverty and their more affluent peers in terms of opportunities to learn. Teachers who hold misconceptions of poverty and people living in poverty tend to blame families for their socioeconomic circumstances and students for underachievement. In Gorski's (2012) words, "[W]e cannot hope to provide the best possible educational experiences to students from families in poverty without a willingness to reject stereotypes and prejudices" (p. 314).

VOICES FROM POVERTY

JAVON

I was born in a small town in the South. For the most part, we were raised by a single mother. She had five boys, no girls. Two of those boys, myself and my brother, are twins. One of the things that I saw very early on was that the living conditions were substandard. That was very easy for me to pick up on as a little boy.

I remember my mom, bless her heart, walking. We used to walk across town just to go to the library; there wasn't a car. And I remember my great aunt, who was an alcoholic.

Even back to the days of kindergarten and 1st grade, there was not a whole lot to give. So even though we were not well off from a resource standpoint, we received the love and the lessons that needed to be taught to young children. We spent a lot of time with my Auntie while my mom was working two, three jobs.

Auntie used to make sure that we had pencil boxes with pencils and crayons. Your pencil box was a King Edward cigar box. One of the things that my Auntie used to say is,

"Education is important. You have no excuse. You have tools in your hand. Go out there, go to school, act right, and get all you can learn right now so you can live better than we live." I believed these folks because I recognized that their living conditions were not ideal.

Mom worked at a foundry that my twin brother and I used to walk past. The foundry is surrounded by fencing, and my mother used to throw us change over the fence. It still brings tears to my eyes to this day. My mother at one point said, "Son, you've got to get your education so you don't have to work like this."

We understood very early the lesson that if you are going to make it and if you want to live better, you've got to get this now. This is no joke, and you'll have more of a balance, more options than you currently are faced with by getting a quality education.

When we were a little older, my mother went up north to visit some of her family who lived in a small town with a college. She came back home and said, "We're leaving," and there we went. We got on the Greyhound bus. We moved what we could take from all we ever knew. If it didn't go on the Greyhound, it didn't go.

Once we got there, we found folks from all four corners of the world by way of the college. We went to school with kids from Asia, kids from Africa, Europe—all over. Their kids became our peers.

And so you have these little black boys who have been immersed into a melting pot of students coming from well-to-do backgrounds. Many of their parents either worked for the college or they served as professors. As little boys, it was priceless. We would go back to the South to visit, and it would be like, "This cracker this, this white man this." That wasn't in our vernacular; we didn't know that. We knew that through our work, you can be with anybody and be recognized like your peers.

We came from a culture or a background of poverty to the point where we saw things and we'd say, "Hey, man, I don't want my kids to ever have to do that." My mother never put us in harm's way—she was a church lady, a spiritual lady, a smart lady. She worked with what she had. We took our experiences with education and poverty and

they saved us. We took these experiences as children and let them propel us. I let my situational poverty growing up become my propeller, if you will. And I never wanted to be anywhere close to where I was growing up from a situational standpoint.

Early on, the importance of education being the pathway to freedom and to equality was instilled in us by different individuals. When we went up north, we found a place of diversity, a liberal town. Everybody really was appreciated. And I had never seen a black principal. But one of the first people that I saw was a black lady who was our principal at the only elementary school in town. When you see folks like that—they're very prestigious but very professional—you say, "Hey, they look like me. They seem to be pretty happy. That's how I want to be."

And for me, that's how it started to happen. The middle school had a black male principal. I had never been exposed to that. I'd see this clean-cut, dark-skinned man, his beard speckled with grey. Very articulate and well loved by the community. His word was like God; it's like he was a superstar.

In the 4th grade, we had an Asian teacher. She told us, "You guys are special; you guys are going to be somebody." Those folks continued to follow our path and track it, all the way through college.

We used to deliver papers as little boys. This older white couple used to bring us in and give us oatmeal. They used to give us three dollars for a *B* and five dollars for an *A*. They were there until we graduated from college. When my brother graduated with his doctorate in 2006, they were there.

So, we talk about walking a path where we came across individuals who supported us, who encouraged us. I think that played a large key to how I turned out—a teacher and now a principal. And the same for my brothers. And our mom, she did what she needed to do for her boys. She was a strong and resilient woman who guided us to where we are today. ■

4 | DISRUPTION 2: HOLDING HIGH EXPECTATIONS AND PROVIDING NEEDED SUPPORT

Brenna started here when I began teaching 2nd grade. And I remember from the first day she walked into my classroom she was so happy to be in my class. She was excited. She didn't want to leave. She was just ready to learn. And once we started school, I quickly found that she was reading way below grade level. She struggled with accuracy and fluency.

When I met with her parents at a back-to-school potluck, they let me know that she was performing at grade level at her past school. "We never heard anything about these issues." I assured them that we would work to catch her up.

We use guided reading groups. I remember when I pulled her group that first week, she looked at me and said, "I know I am in the lowest reading group," and I said, "I never told you that, Brenna. Why do you think you're in the lowest reading group?" She looked around and said, "Look at their books. They're reading big books. I know this is a little book. I want to be where they are." Every time I tested her, she wanted to know, "OK, I passed. What did I do well? I didn't pass. What do I need to work on?" And every time she didn't pass, she was very hard on herself. I was like, "Brenna, it's OK; we're working on it. We're trying."

Now she is reading at grade level, and she can tell you exactly what she's doing well on and what got her there. If I pull her out for a conference, I feel like she can run my conference for me. She can tell mom and dad, "This is what I'm doing. This is what I need help on." It's a partnership. After I saw that she was so driven, I actually started sharing the data with all my students, individually: "This is what we need to work on," making them very aware of what their next steps needed to be, and just working together to meet them.

—*Marissa, 2nd Grade Teacher*

ANSWERING THE "WHO" QUESTION:
A 100-Word Reflection

*What do you believe about students who live in poverty in terms of their ability to learn? How did you come to believe this?*_____

_____

_____

_____

_____

_____

ANSWERING THE "WHAT" QUESTION:
What the Research Tells Us

Expecting Success: It Matters

By now we hope we have firmly established the idea that success with students who live in poverty depends not only upon the quality of the curriculum and our instruction, but also upon understanding who we are and why we teach (including what we value and believe). In this chapter, we discuss teacher expectations.

You may be tempted to skip the chapter, thinking something like, "I don't need to read this chapter. Of course I believe all kids can learn. I have high expectations for all of them." It is that sort of thinking (which we all do) that makes the topic so difficult. Most of us believe we "expect success" from all students. Certainly, almost every mission statement written in schools and districts explicitly states the belief that *all* students can learn. To really tackle this topic and open ourselves to learning something new, we have to be willing to go to a place we rarely go—to the beliefs and values that we unconsciously hold about ourselves and about our students and their ability or inability to learn.

We have an extensive knowledge base about teacher expectations, which gives us a "rich source of theory, research, and debate" about how to create the best environment for disadvantaged students (Good & Nichols, 2001, p. 114). Nearly 50 years ago, Ray Rist (1970) and colleagues conducted an ethnographic study that followed 1st graders for three years in a high-poverty school in St. Louis. They found that teacher expectations established in 1st grade and observed in the grouping schemes, the quality of instruction provided, and the nature and scope of student-teacher interactions were replicated well beyond 1st grade. Although education is often purported to be the great equalizer in society, Rist's study indicated just the opposite. He demonstrated that a type of "caste" system develops within classrooms and schools that later emerges in society as a "class" system (p. 299).

Rist's study was first published in the *Harvard Education Review* in 1970; however, in 2000, 30 years after publication, the editorial board selected it for republication because they wanted to "encourage all of us to think about the work that remains in creating a just and equitable educational experience for all children" (Rist, 2000, p. 257). In his reintroduction to the study, Rist asserted, "The sobering reality is that when it comes to both color and class, U.S. schools tend to *conform* much more to the contours of American society than they *transform* it. And, this appears to be a lesson that we are not wanting to learn" (p. 260, emphasis added).

Rist (2000) claimed, "The success of an educational institution and any individual teacher should not be measured by the treatment of the high-achieving students, but rather by the treatment of those not achieving" (p. 299). Does Rist's claim bring forward in our minds all the factors we do not control in students' lives? Are we OK with his claim? Do we agree? The teachers we interviewed and the schools we studied demonstrate that schools do not have to reproduce the inequities in society; but these teachers and schools do remain the outliers in the system, which reminds us a lot of work remains to be done. That work begins with each of us. Here is the bottom line: what we expect of our students matters; it matters a lot.

Expectancy Studies: Two Kinds of Effects

Researchers have studied two kinds of teacher-expectancy effects extensively: sustaining effects (Entwisle, Alexander, & Olson, 1998; Rist, 1970) and self-fulfilling prophecy effects (Brophy, 1982; Good & Nichols, 2001; Rosenthal & Jacobson, 1968).

Sustaining Effects

In addition to Rist's 1970 study, others have shown that expectations set early in students' schooling can predict their subsequent performance. Grades earned by students in 1st grade have been found to be a "more reliable bellwether" of a student's future performance than test scores (Entwisle, Alexander, & Olson, 1998, p. 12). A sustaining effect occurs "when teachers expect students to continue to act or perform according to previously established patterns and may disregard contradictory evidence of change" (Rubie Davies, Hattie, & Hamilton, 2006, p 430). Too often we become "well adjusted" to our expectations (Brophy, 1982, p. 48).

What we believe about our students' potential influences both what we attend to and how we interpret events. When a student for whom a teacher holds low expectations does succeed, the teacher may not recognize it. Rather, the teacher may attribute the success to coincidence or a chance occurrence, or may be suspicious of the outcome, believing the student may have cheated or copied others' work. Teachers who have "given up" on students can feel threatened by success they did not expect (Brophy, 1982).

Self-Fulfilling Prophecy Effects

Self-fulfilling prophecy effects occur "when an initially erroneous belief leads to its fulfillment" (Rubie-Davies, Hattie, & Hamilton, 2006, p. 430). The initial belief can be positive and desirable or negative and undesirable. Self-fulfilling prophecy effect happens when a teacher develops a set of beliefs about a student based on a variety of factors. Those beliefs influence how the teacher interacts with the student, and in turn, the student comes to expect similar treatment in the future, behaving in ways that mirrors the teacher's expectations. When the student responds in a manner that is consistent with the teacher's beliefs, the teacher's expectations (high or low) are reinforced. Students interpret the teacher's expectations as "self-revealing" and begin to align their self-image with those expectations (Darley & Fazio, 1980, in Brophy, 1982, p. 57).

In the case of self-fulfilling prophecy, then, a change in student performance can be created based on our expectation of that student. Sustained effects thwart the potential for any change because our initial expectations for a student may blind us to the student's subsequent success. Mary, who teaches special education, understood the powerful impact her expectations had on her students. She explained, "I've told them, 'I don't care where you are. I don't care what the paper says. I don't care what other people have said about you. Whatever you want to do, you can do it. You just have to put your mind to it, and I will help you.'"

Influences on Teachers' Expectations

Researchers do not completely understand how teachers form their expectations; however, they do know, in addition to academic and behavioral performance, teachers consider information related to a variety of individual student attributes when setting expectations, including race, gender, class, labels, stereotypes, language, personality, attractiveness, age, social skills, knowledge of students' background, and factors related to parents/families/caregivers.

In establishing expectations for students, Gregory and Huang (2013) assert, "it cannot be ruled out" that implicit bias or unconscious stereotypes may also influence our expectations (p. 52). Several studies have concluded that even when academic achievement is the same, teachers tend to have lower expectations of their students of color and those who live in poverty (Beady & Hansell, 1981; Nichols & Good, 2004; Rubie-Davies, Hattie, & Hamilton, 2006; Solomon, Battistich, & Hom, 1996). Gregory and Huang (2013) found that teachers held higher expectations for Asian students in terms of going to college, even when those students were comparable to their peers in socioeconomic status and achievement.

High expectations matter more for students of color and those who live in poverty. Students of color tend to be more susceptible than their white peers to teachers' expectations (McKown & Weinstein, 2002; Nichols & Good, 2004; Steele & Aronson, 1995). Internalizing a teacher's belief in their potential can provide a protective factor for students, which can help counter other risk factors in their lives (Gregory & Huang, 2013). The greater the risk factors in a student's life, the more high expectations matter to the student's life chances (Wood et al., 2011, in Gregory & Huang, 2013).

In examining whether or not the teacher's race influences expectations of students, one study demonstrated that black teachers and white teachers held the same expectations for success in elementary and secondary schooling; however, black teachers expected more of their black students in terms of going to college than did white teachers (Beady & Hansell, 1981); and in another study, teachers whose race was other than black were 12 percentage points less likely to expect black students to complete a four-year college degree than teachers who were black (Gershenson, Holt, Papageorge, 2015). Nonetheless, other scholars claim the race of the teacher is not necessarily the critical variable (Ferguson, 1998, as cited in Good & Nichols, 2001), asserting teachers of any race may need support in understanding the challenges faced by students from disadvantaged homes.

How Low Expectations Contribute to Opportunity Gaps and Achievement Gaps

Holding low expectations of students contributes to gaps in learning and achievement primarily through the types of learning opportunities teachers provide students (Weinstein, 2002). To illustrate, although studies have consistently demonstrated that constructivist approaches are effective with students who live in poverty (Haberman, 1991; Knapp, Shields, & Turnbull, 1995), such pedagogy is least often used (Solomon, Battistich, & Hom, 1996). Teachers with low expectations use a more controlling pedagogy that is a less engaging, less constructivist, and less challenging approach to teaching (Good & Nichols, 2001; Haberman, 1991; Solomon, Battistich, & Hom, 1996). Demanding little from students, a control-oriented approach is often reflected in an unspoken contract between teachers and students that entails something like this: "I won't expect much from you, and in return you won't give me much trouble. Is it a deal?"

Protecting students out of "concern" for them is another way in which low expectations contribute to gaps in opportunity and achievement. Mary confessed to us that she "once had been an enabler" and advised those who wish to be more successful with students who live in poverty to "always be reflective" about one's practice. Teachers call on students for whom they hold lower expectations less frequently and are more critical of those students when they provide incorrect answers (Brophy & Good, 1970). In addition, although they tend to be aware they are calling on these students less often, they can be less aware of the nature of their interactions when they do call on them (Good & Brophy, 1974). Teachers can be reluctant to ask challenging questions to students for whom they hold low expectations for fear of embarrassing them. Also, they can be too quick to provide the answer without letting those students engage in a productive struggle to understand the content (Good & Nichols, 2001).

Conflating feedback related to a student's behavior with feedback on their potential as a learner is another way in which low expectations have been found to contribute to gaps. Of course, many students need productive feedback about both their behavior and their academic learning; however, "it is critical that teachers deliver such information without lowering students' beliefs about their value and potential as learners" (Good & Nichols, 2001, p. 123). We have seen this phenomenon play out in high-poverty schools when teachers punish students by lowering their grade for what was in essence a behavioral issue. At other times, teachers simply spend less time providing feedback to students with behavioral challenges, sending a message to students that they are not valued as learners. This teacher behavior can become a self-fulfilling prophecy. Figure 4.1 summarizes how teachers' actions in the classroom differ depending on whether they hold high or low expectations of students.

Students who have been given a daily dose of teacher-centered, low-cognitive-demand instruction for even a short number of years may be resistant to higher expectations (Haberman, 2012); therefore, it is important that teachers who set high expectations for *all* their students establish trusting relationships (see Chapter 3) and work to fully engage students in the learning process. Even then, persistence and insistence are likely to be necessary until students begin to get intrinsic rewards from schooling. Again, Mary offered some advice, saying, "Be compassionate and caring, but also be firm. Don't lower your expectations." Additionally, she has found authentic goal setting to be a powerfully motivating strategy. "[I]f kids know what they're learning, and why, or what they're supposed to learn, they're more likely to learn it."

Student and Parental Expectations

At this point you may be wondering about the role student and parental expectations play in student success. These expectations are important and can have an additive effect. For example, taken together, high expectations on the part of teachers, students, and parents are a stronger predictor of success in postsecondary education than are a students' academic performance or socioeconomic status (Gregory & Huang, 2013). Nonetheless,

FIGURE 4.1 | Low Versus High Expectations:
A Comparison of Teacher Behavior

Teachers Who Hold Low Expectations	Teachers Who Hold High Expectations
• Call on student(s) less frequently • Provide less "wait time" for answers • Provide answers or call on another student without wait time • Reward low-quality or incorrect answers • Criticize more frequently for failure • Praise less for success • Provide less informative feedback on performance • Interact less frequently • Seat students far away from teacher • Provide less "benefit of the doubt" in borderline cases • Rely on tasks with low levels of cognitive demand • Overuse of independent/seat work • Use less friendly nonverbal behavior	• Articulate the belief that student can achieve at high levels • Create warm social-emotional relationships focused on strengths, funds of knowledge, cultural understandings, and interests/aspirations • Provide informative feedback on performance to scaffold learning • Teach content and use tasks with high cognitive demand • Ask frequent, high-level questions • Encourage a productive struggle (refraining from giving answers, allowing wait time, guiding to answer) • Maintain close physical proximity • Interact frequently • Use positive nonverbal communication

Sources: For low expectations: Allington, 1980; Babad, 2009; Brophy & Good, 1970; Good & Nichols, 2001; Haberman, 1991, 2012; Kleinfeld, 1975; Solomon, Dattistich, & Hom, 1996. For high expectations: Barr & Gibson, 2013; Brophy, 1982; Good & Nichols, 2001; Haberman, 1991, 2012; Harris & Rosenthal, 1985; Johnston, 2012; Kleinfeld, 1975; Rosenthal, 1974; Solomon, Battistich, & Hom, 1996; Weinstein, 2002.

students who live in poverty, particularly generational poverty, may depend more upon teachers to help them see alternatives for their future than do their more affluent peers (Milner, 2015). Although parents or caregivers may have aspirations for their children to do well in school and continue their education, as Good and Nichols (2001) point out, "Parents who are coping with various issues may have little time to mediate low teacher expectations for their children" (p. 119). Depending upon their own educational experience, they may or may not be able to mentor their children. As Anna, a teacher who grew up in poverty and lived on her own throughout high school, explains,

> Starting in high school, when all that stuff was going on in my life [both parents incarcerated on drug charges], I wouldn't have even known if I could go

to college. I didn't know if I could afford it. That is why it is important that we show students, "Yes, you can. You can get somewhere."

Richard Milner (2015), in his book *Rac(e)ing to Class,* calls students such as Anna "school-dependent" students. These students depend more upon school than their more affluent peers not only for basic needs, but also "to help them understand, navigate, and function in school" (p. 49). For such students, teacher expectations become even more important. Anna, who was placed in special education until she was in high school, describes what she tells her students:

> I want to ... show them that [they] may be in SPED now, but it doesn't mean that [they're] going to be there forever. I tell them, "You may struggle now, but if you work hard you can get past that and get to where you want to go. It may be harder. I know I had to study a lot harder than probably a lot of other people, but I was able to do it."

Holding high expectations for students living in poverty also means fostering in them human agency—the belief and knowledge that we can make choices and take action to influence the conditions or circumstances in our life. Living in the trauma of poverty, students can come to believe they have very little control over their lives (Beegle, 2007). In addition to setting high expectations for behavior and academics, Celia told us she uses poetry to develop personal agency in her students.

> I have certain poems that I have them memorize that I just love. We recite it and we analyze it. We talk about what each line means. "Life Doesn't Frighten Me at All" by Dr. [Maya] Angelou—I love to teach the kids and memorize that one. Oh, and then there was another one that I loved to do years ago about the critic—"Don't Listen to the Critic." We would memorize that one and analyze it ... and I've seen kids transform.

No doubt it is most beneficial when everyone holds high expectations—teacher, parent, and student. However, that may not be the case for students living in poverty. The good news is that teacher expectations have been shown to have the greatest predictive power (Gregory & Huang, 2013), and those expectations are within our control. Celia's words were indicative of the sentiment expressed by all of the teachers we interviewed.

I set the expectation. I clearly define it, and then I just hold them to it. Along the way, I encourage them… and constantly tell them, "I believe in you. I believe in you. I'm not going to quit on you. I know you can do it."

When Teachers Raise Their Expectations

When teachers who hold low expectations are provided opportunities for professional learning and constructive feedback, they can change their expectations of their students and their response to them (Good & Nichols, 2001; Rubie-Davies, 2015; Weinstein et al., 1991). For instance, in one study, seven teachers were supported with job-embedded professional development to implement "positive expectancy practices," which included the following: an improved curriculum, heterogeneous groupings, increased methods for assessment, use of cooperative teaching approaches, encouraging more student-centered activities, fostering greater engagement in school events, and developing warm student-teacher relationships, as well as positive relationships with parents.

This group was matched with a "control group" of teachers who did not receive the professional development. Student engagement and academic achievement greatly increased in the classes taught by the teachers who had the opportunity to expand their professional repertoire. Additionally, students in these classes reported being more excited about learning. Students who had formerly been labeled and assigned to the lowest tracks were achieving at levels similar to students in the honors track. In the end, the school abolished tracking; however, in the following year, when the students in the experimental group were assigned to new teachers who had not received the job-embedded professional development, the academic gains were not maintained (Weinstein, 2002).

Rubie-Davies and colleagues (2015) demonstrated a similar finding. Teachers were provided professional development in practices used by "high-expectations teachers"—specifically, flexible grouping, goal setting, and improved classroom climate. These teachers and their students were compared to a control group. "The gain [in mathematics] in comparison with the control group was the equivalent of students increasing their scores by an additional three months over the course of the academic year (28 percent)" (p. 10). Both studies demonstrate that when supported to increase their repertoire of instructional skills and sense of efficacy, teachers raise their expectations of students, resulting in positive outcomes.

Estella spoke to the importance of teacher expectations when she said,

> I think if you're really committed to the work, you understand you are accountable. Every day you wake up as a teacher you have the opportunity to make a difference in someone's life. You have to believe that. My greatest challenge is not the children; it is having the other adults in the building see what I see in the children. I want people to see beyond what's there and see the potential, because I believe that is what my teachers did for me. They saw what I could be in the future. They poured it into me.

An Important Distinction:
Where Students Are and Where They Can Go

Studies have found that most educators' perceptions of students are accurate and based on the best data and information available (Brophy, 1982). Their ability to be flexible in their perceptions and change their expectations based on new information has also been demonstrated (Good & Brophy, 1974), and this competency is vital when working with under-achieving students. In their preparation programs, most teachers likely learned the importance of accurately assessing students and guiding their instruction based on that assessment. Understanding and attending to the tension between accurately assessing where students are (academically, behaviorally, and in social-emotional terms) and holding high expectations for where they can go is an important aspect of establishing a poverty-disrupting classroom culture.

Teachers we interviewed, and others we have talked with throughout the United States, have shared stories of students who tackle seemingly insurmountable obstacles when teachers believe in them, set high expectations for them, provide them with a rich pedagogy, help them to establish goals, and support them in believing in themselves. They have told us about students who exit special education programs after years of pull-out services, even self-contained services. We have heard about students who begin the year with a legacy of not meeting the standards on the state's standardized achievement tests only to finish the year "exceeding proficiency." There are the stories about the first-generation students who go to college, although it was "never on their radar screens" before a teacher said, "You're really good at _____. Have you thought about college?" As Javon told us,

> We preach to kids that, "Hey, [what has happened in the past] is just situational. It is what it is. Time is just a picture. Now you can change that frame every second. What is it that you're choosing to do?" And with high expectations these kids could do anything they want, period.

 ## ANSWERING THE "HOW" QUESTION:
Tips from Teachers

Seven Practical Suggestions for Holding High Expectations

Holding high expectations for every student is predicated on a belief in the human potential for growth and development. In what follows we have condensed the ideas and strategies teachers have shared with us into seven tips for holding high expectations for all your students.

1. Build on Relationships to Make Learning Relevant

Anna, to whom you were introduced in Chapter 3, told us,

> I can relate to a lot of these students—those who have parents who have been incarcerated—because I grew up in that situation. I became a teacher because I thought, "Well, maybe someday I can actually make an impact on these students and show them that you can come from nothing and achieve everything they want to."

Whether or not you grew up in poverty, holding high expectations for students and supporting them in meeting those expectations begins with the topic we discussed in Chapter 3—caring relationships. Students will work hard to meet the expectations set by a teacher they like and respect, and who they know has their best interests at heart.

Additionally, students are likely to put forth their best effort when they are being asked to engage in learning activities that are relevant to them. To know what is relevant to our students we must know them well.

As we discussed in Chapter 3, the teachers we spoke with used a variety of strategies to get to know their students, and in many cases this knowledge helped them make academic content more relevant to students' cultures, interests, and aspirations. For example, they conducted home visits, interviewed parents to capture their insights into their children, interviewed students, engaged in dialogue journaling with their students, and asked students to complete surveys related to personal interests, passions, and aspirations. They then intentionally linked this information to students' academic learning whenever possible, including selecting books, choosing writing topics, determining a project-based learning focus, placing students in internships and apprenticeships, setting personal academic goals, and determining career pathways, to name a few.

Some schools take a schoolwide approach to making "school learning" relevant to students' lives. One school asks students to develop a Personal Education Plan (PEP) based on their passions and aspirations for the future. Other schools use specific programs and approaches to make school more relevant by infusing student voice into school culture and curriculum, as well as tapping into their aspirations (see www.qisa.org). Nearly every teacher we interviewed talked about the importance of helping students who live in poverty to envision an alternative future for themselves. This is accomplished, in part, by helping students connect education to a possible life trajectory, which begins with knowing their dreams and aspirations.

2. Provide for Rigor and Risk Taking

Teachers who succeed with students who live in poverty use a pedagogy that is consistent with what research tells us about how people learn (Bransford et al., 2000). In poverty-disrupting classrooms, students are asked to take an inquiry stance, using logic and reasoning to construct meaning and to solve problems. Learning *activities* are just that—students are *actively* engaged in doing something for real and relevant purposes. Lectures and worksheets are kept to a minimum.

Students may resist your use of such pedagogy, although your instruction may be more interesting and engaging, particularly if they have grown accustomed to the unspoken contract in which little has been expected of them, as we described previously in this chapter. Nonetheless, such resistance can be overcome. After spending time intentionally building relationships with her students, Lizzy capitalizes on their interests and curiosity using student-centered, constructivist approaches with an expectation of some initial resistance from students. As she explained,

> I never lower my expectation. When I teach Project Lead the Way, it is probably one of the most rigorous courses that I teach in this kind of school [high-poverty] because our students are accustomed to being spoon-fed information. Project Lead the Way is student led and student centered, and requires them to have an inquiry-based approach. And so, they're not accustomed to having things at their fingertips and being able to utilize those things. They're used to being able to raise their hand and have the teacher solve the problem.

Providing support for students to meet high expectations in the context of inquiry-based, constructivist classrooms requires us to teach students that "failure" or "mistakes" are an expected part of the process. When was the last time you explicitly taught your students that failure is part of the learning process? When we asked Celia what advice she would give teachers attempting to create a poverty-disrupting classroom, she said,

> Even when students fail, tell them it's OK. You didn't get it? No big deal. We'll keep working on it—allowing them to fail and making it OK to fail. Don't ask for perfection; ask for their best effort.

Students who live in poverty often come to school with fewer readiness-to-learn skills than their more affluent peers, and unfortunately the gap typically widens as they progress through the grades. Too often they view themselves as "failures" at an early age and eventually develop many coping skills for avoiding embarrassment. In poverty-disrupting classrooms, rigor and risk taking are linked. Setting and supporting high expectations entails normalizing failure and making it safe for learners to take risks. In addition to normalizing failure, developing a community of learners among the students supports risk taking. Miranda explained,

> I have seven expectations in my class, and one of them is "We all make mistakes." That includes me. I give an example of how I make a mistake and it's OK. We all make mistakes, we try our best, we celebrate each other's success, we do everything with pride; we are a team.

3. Be a "Warm Demander": Insistent and Supportive

Mary described herself as a "nag," saying,

> There was one girl… she was just ready to give up and throw in the towel. And I actually had her brother at the elementary school, and when I moved over to the high school, I had her. I had a relationship with her mom and her brother. So I knew the family…. I just kept telling her, "You can do this; you can do this; I'll help you. Come to my room, we'll do this together." And she told me that she wouldn't have graduated if I hadn't stayed on her. She was like, "If you hadn't told me that I can do it and didn't stay on me about it, I would have just quit. I would have said forget it…." Yes, I'm a great nag. I just keep on them, on all the students. I nag all of them until they walk across the stage.

We would describe Mary as a "Warm Demander." Judy Kleinfeld (1975) coined the term in her portrayal of effective teachers of Athabaskan Indian and Eskimo students in Alaska, and Franita Ware (2006) used it to illustrate the attributes of effective teachers of African American students, describing such teachers as those who respond with proactive attitudes toward students of color and have strong, positive racial identity (p. 451). Warm Demanders challenge students equally, moving beyond simply believing students can learn to insisting they learn and providing the necessary supports for them to do so (Ware, 2006).

Such teachers may appear "harsh" to "uninformed observers" (Bondy & Ross, 2008); however, a closer look reveals their unconditional positive regard (Rogers, 1957) for every student and an insistence on mutual respect. They have a "no excuses" philosophy and a belief in the capacity of individuals to succeed; they do not engage in power struggles with students, nor do they threaten or demean them (Bondy & Ross, 2008). Because they know students well, they are able to address individual needs, often providing an extended family-like relationship described as "other mothering" (Ware, 2006, p. 444). In preparing to write this book, we interviewed many teachers whom we would describe as Warm Demanders.

4. Act from an Empathic Perspective

Empathy is a disposition one can choose to adopt. Studies have demonstrated that an empathic disposition not only leads to better relationships with students (see Chapter 3), but also promotes a supportive classroom climate for student-centered pedagogy (McAllister & Irvine, 2002). Empathic behavior is characterized as "sensitivity, patience, respect, tolerance, acceptance, understanding, flexibility, openness, and humility" (p. 439).

An empathic disposition is important not only when establishing high expectations for academic learning, but also for other forms of learning such as social skills, productive habits of mind, and positive behavior. Most of the teachers we interviewed told us empathy was a key to their success with students. Miranda's point of view was indicative of others. She shared her perspective:

> When you know your students and your students know you, you don't need to have all the rules and you won't need to raise your voice. I talk to them as I'm talking to you, and they'll listen to what I'm saying because they know that I respect them for who they are as people. I don't talk to them like they're little kids. I talk to them as people. I may not use big words, but I talk to them on a level that lets them know I respect them and I expect the same in return, and they do.

Stanford University researchers Okonofua, Paunesku, and Walton (2016) found that when teachers adopted an empathic mindset for discipline, student suspension rates were cut in half, respect for teachers was sustained, and students were motivated to behave well in class. Teachers in the study who received a modest amount of professional development focused on developing an empathic mindset regarding discipline, which was defined as "valu[ing] students' perspective and maintaining high-quality relationships during disciplinary interactions" (p. 5221). Understanding and valuing students' perspectives "does not ask teachers to share students' perspective or to think that perspective is reasonable" (p. 5223). An empathic mindset is based on the premise that when teachers are successful in conveying their respect and care for students, the students' "feelings about, and behavior in, school can and do improve" (p. 5223). In an interview in *Education Week* (Sparks, 2016), one of the researchers, Jason Okonofua, asserted, "Changing the mindset of one teacher can change the social experience of that child's entire world."

5. Hold a Growth Mindset and Encourage the Same in Students

In his book *Opening Minds: Using Language to Change Lives,* Peter Johnston (2012) describes two belief systems that influence how we, as teachers and as students, view intelligence and what it means to "know" something. Drawing on Carol Dweck's (2006) research, he describes the two belief systems as "dynamic" and "fixed." When individuals have a dynamic perspective, "they think of ability, or intelligence, as something that grows with learning and depends on the situation" (p. 11). On the other hand, when they have a fixed perspective, they view intelligence as "a character trait, something people have more or less of, usually from birth." Although "holding a fixed theory or a dynamic theory may seem like no big deal... when people run into difficulties [learning, completing a task, and so on], their theories matter big time" (p. 11). He elaborates,

> When children holding fixed theories encounter difficulties, mistakes become crippling. Worse, if they think that a task might be difficult, they choose not to even try so that they won't fail and maybe look stupid. They choose not to try even if it means losing an opportunity to learn something important. They choose, instead, to look good, or at least not look bad, at whatever they are doing. (p. 11)

As we described in Chapter 2, for Donna Beegle (2007) and those she studied, growing up in poverty was a deeply shaming experience. Many came to believe they were fated and they had little agency to change their lives. They also viewed failure as inevitable and spoke of deficiencies being inherent (p. 55). Students who live in poverty and underachieve may have a fixed-ability mindset and have "learned" that they would rather misbehave, passively resist, or give up quickly than "look stupid."

In poverty-disruptive classrooms, teachers foster a dynamic theory of intelligence, learning, and knowing. Johnston (2012) suggests three ways teachers influence such a perspective in students: (1) what they choose to say when students are successful or unsuccessful (feedback and praise), (2) the manner in which they frame activities, and (3) "what [they] explicitly teach children about how people's brains and minds work" (p. 18). He goes on to assert that how teachers give feedback to students, although the hardest factor for teachers to change, may be the greatest leverage point. Feedback, he suggests, should be "process-oriented" or "effort-oriented" rather than "person-oriented" (p. 38). Restating what the student did or did not do and then providing suggestions for how the student might approach the task differently is providing process-oriented feedback. Conversely, attaching a judgment of good or bad to the student without explanation of why the performance was good or bad is person-oriented feedback.

It is not uncommon for teachers to think the problem for students who live in poverty and underachieve is one of self-esteem, believing that praise will raise such students' self-esteem. Despite the shame that has been attached to living in poverty in society, we assert the problem is not so much self-esteem as lack of personal agency—the belief in our ability to act on behalf of our own life. As Johnston (2012) points out, providing feedback with statements such as "I like the way you…" turns the focus to the process but also provides a form of praise that is "not helpful," as it infers the students' effort is for the purpose of pleasing the teacher. Feedback that is process-oriented without the praise "turn[s] students' attention to process and away from fixed-theory explanations" for the purpose of building their sense of agency (p. 42). Johnston suggests, as an example, that a teacher might say,

> "When you added dialogue to your piece, I really understood how Amy [the character] felt." This is not so much praise as a causal statement—you did this [added dialogue], with this consequence [I understood how the character felt]. Causal process statements are at the heart of building agency (p. 42)

When we interviewed Leslie, she described how she saw her 1st graders transform throughout the year into self-directed learners:

> They'll work hard, and they'll rise to the occasion. I ask, "Do you think you did your best? Do you want to try again?" And then they make that choice that "Yes, I should probably try again because I scribbled through this and it's terrible and you can't read it." And they feel successful, and empowered. And they feel in control of what they're doing.

In a poverty-disruptive classroom, supporting all students to meet high expectations, particularly those who live in poverty and underachieve, entails fostering an environment in which fixed mindsets are challenged (by what we as teachers say and do) for the purpose of helping students to re-envision themselves as people with potential and agency.

6. Interrogate Your Mental Map

Many of the scholars who have studied the effect of teacher expectations on student outcomes acknowledge that most teachers accurately assess students' current level of learning; nonetheless, they call upon educators "to examine their beliefs, stereotypes, and consequent expectations to see if these could be variables that ultimately affect students' life chances" (Rubie-Davies, Hattie, & Hamilton, 2006, p. 442). Our expectations of our students are fundamentally concerned not with the present, but with the future. They are a reflection of the potential we see in each student.

Two starting points for reflection on your mental map might be the stereotypes we address in this book and your beliefs about intelligence, learning, and knowing. Are you guided by a belief that these things are fixed or dynamic? Johnston (2012) claims,

> Indeed, people who take up fixed theorizing form stereotypes more quickly than those choosing dynamic theorizing; they are more inclined to apply trait thinking in describing group members, and they make more extreme trait judgments, whether positive or negative. In fact, people choosing fixed theorizing focus on information that confirms their stereotypes, ignoring disconfirming information. The more information goes against their stereotype, such as a poor, low-achieving boy doing well on a test, the less attention they give to that information. Within a fixed theory, once a student is judged as lazy (or friendly or learning disabled, etc.) we start to see evidence of it everywhere in their behavior. Their situation and psychological processes, such as intentions and feelings, take a back seat. (p. 19)

Acknowledging the adverse effects poverty can have on learning, poverty-disrupting teachers understand that each student is affected differently by poverty. They are willing to interrogate their mental maps to ensure their own biases do not place limits on their students. For James, such interrogation entailed "asking some pretty hard questions of myself and the system to identify the factors that actually create the bigger injustices later." He continued,

> It's asking some of those questions and addressing it on our small scale. I think schools have great potential for supporting meaningful growth in human beings to build a better world, right? I mean to build a better society. The society that we choose to build as opposed to just what we receive.... I think so often we just receive, we don't question. I think we all need to ask

ourselves reflective questions—I don't know if it's enough. I don't know if it's ever going to be enough, but it's what I can do.

7. Employ the 4Cs:
Caring, Clear, and Consistent Communication of Expectations

Caring, clear, and consistent communication of our expectations is part of creating a classroom culture that disrupts poverty. Teachers described numerous ways in which they communicated their expectations. Some expectations were cocreated with students and others were not. Often teachers described how they visually display their expectations in their classrooms and the frequency with which they referenced them. Getting "on the same page" in terms of expectations with parents and caregivers was also important to many. The following are 10 ways to ensure expectations are clear and consistent:

1. Cocreate the expectations with students, when appropriate to promote ownership.

2. Coestablish learning goals with each student to support greater engagement.

3. Use rubrics and exemplars to make academic outcomes concrete.

4. Establish routines and structures for classroom management; model, teach, and practice them.

5. Teach academic discourse and provide opportunities for group learning to use it.

6. Use student-led conferencing with portfolio development to promote metacognition.

7. Develop a sense of community in which students can articulate expectations to each other and hold each other accountable.

8. Integrate student self-assessment into academic and social-emotional learning to encourage introspection.

9. Explicitly "normalize" failure, productive struggle, and revision as part of the learning process.

10. Use visual displays as a source of reference to promote consistency.

Engaging students in deeply understanding their expectations was critical, teachers told us. They used strategies and tools such as modeling, goal setting, peer reviews, rubrics, student work samples, and conferencing not only to communicate their expectations, but also to engage students in setting personal expectations for their own learning. Marissa described how she both communicated her expectations to students during Writers Workshop and engaged them in improving their learning.

> I model. I do a lot of think-out-louds, and I show the steps. I ask for ideas from other students, and I let them know that it's OK to get ideas from other students. They have the rubrics at their desk, and they also put them in their books that they can refer to. It lets them see what a level 4, what a level 3, what a level 2 and 1 all have in each section. We conference, and I give them suggestions, I give them positive comments; and from there we grade it together, and then students always ask me after we're done, "Well, can I change this to be a level 4?" They add things to their writing, and they come back and say, "Can you read it again?" And I give them more feedback.

For students who live in poverty, a teacher's expectations can make or break them. See Figure 4.2 for some additional specific suggestions for communicating high expectations. Seeing beyond the poverty to the potential provides a protective factor that can make a significant difference in improved outcomes for students and is one of the many ways teachers ensure equity, which is the focus of the next chapter.

APPLYING YOUR LEARNING TO YOUR PRACTICE

- Think of a time when you had to learn something that you were afraid was too hard or you weren't sure you were "smart enough" to learn. How did you feel? What did you need from others? What happened?
- What assumptions did you hold about your own intelligence?
- Describe the attributes of a student who is underperforming yet has the potential to learn.
- Think about two students—one who is succeeding in school and one who is underachieving. Compare and contrast the dialogue you have with each of these students.

- In your school, how do educators talk about students who live in poverty? How does this influence what educators believe about their intelligence and potential?
- Think about a student who lives in poverty and is underachieving. How does that student "explain" himself or herself as a learner (in terms of such things as ability to complete assignments, engage in activities, take tests, complete homework)? How do you respond to the student?

FIGURE 4.2 | Ideas for Communicating High Expectations

Publicize Your Expectations—From the first day of school, have your expectations posted around the classroom. For example, one teacher posted what she called the "Seven Expectations of Highly Effective Students," and focused on the seven expectations by teaching, modeling, and having students practice them in the first two weeks of school.

Send a Letter—Send a letter to each student outlining your general expectations, but also include a personal statement or two about your belief in them and your willingness to be there to support them.

Dialogue Journals—Use dialogue journals for clarifying expectations based on the individual needs of students. Let them know that, as part of the journaling process, they can ask questions if they are confused or do not understand something.

Co-Construction—Involve students in setting the expectations. Students write down (on sticky notes) their ideas for their role and responsibilities in the classroom, and you do the same. The students then post the sticky notes on a large piece of butcher paper. The students read what their classmates wrote and then take part in a class discussion to come to agreement and establish expectations. The guiding question is "Why do rules exist?" The activity serves as the basis for how students and you will act as a community of learners, and a poster-sized version of the list of expectations remains displayed in the classroom for reference.

Feedback: Let Me Count the Ways—Provide feedback to students in multiple ways—written comments, verbal comments, peer review with comments, rubrics, and conferencing.

Positive Presuppositions—A positive orientation toward students' potential is key. Whether you are positive or negative, your orientation is contagious.

Teacher Talk for Student Agency—Be cautious about how you give praise. Use praise to emphasize what the student has accomplished rather than connecting it to "pleasing the teacher." Use language to extol the virtues of effort and reinforce a growth mindset. Teach students how to engage in academic discourse, and provide "low-risk" opportunities for all students to participate. Use language that encourages self-discipline and self-governance. Two great resources are *The Power of Our Words: Teacher Language That Helps Children Learn*, by Paula Denton, and *Opening Minds: Using Language to Change Lives*, by Peter H. Johnston.

Let Students Take the Wheel—Implementing student-led conferencing supports students in coming to view themselves as powerful agents in their own learning. Well-designed student-led conferences between students, parents/families, and teachers require students to identify their own strengths and challenges and to demonstrate what they know and how they know it.

Application of Learning Matrix

To help you apply what you are learning to your professional practice, see Appendix A. Each chapter's high-leverage question is listed there, with space to list each student and reflect on what you know. Teachers with more than 25 students may want to use multiple matrices or select a particular class period. For this chapter, here is the high-leverage question: What do I expect _____ [student's name] to accomplish this year?

Challenging Our Mental Maps:
Learning, Unlearning, and Relearning Summary Table

Pause for a few minutes and use the following questions to consider your current thinking as it relates to the information and ideas presented in this chapter.

Learning: What conceptions did you hold about teacher expectations before reading this chapter?

Unlearning: How, if at all, did the chapter challenge your beliefs or thinking?

Relearning: How might this "challenge to your thinking" or new idea be beneficial or helpful to you?

Action: What *action* will you take, and why?

As you consider your answers and progress through this book, record your answers for each chapter in the summary table supplied in Appendix B. The summary table provides you with a model for exploring your mental map, reflecting on current practice, developing your theory of action, and planning next steps.

 ## COMMUNITIES OF PRACTICE:
Extending Your Learning with Others

- How can we use the information in the chapter to ensure high expectations are held for all students in our school?
- How can we share information with parents about the importance of holding high expectations for their children?
- How can we help each other address myths and stereotypes related to students who live in poverty?

- Have we used any of the suggestions for holding high expectations for our students recommended in this chapter? If so, how have they worked? What other suggestions can we offer each other?

Challenging Stereotypes to Hold High Expectations

Research clearly demonstrates the importance of teacher expectations and specifically points to the role implicit bias can play; so our willingness to challenge our mental map, particularly our biases, is critical. Two stereotypes that may pose barriers to holding high expectations for all our students are the beliefs that people living in poverty are lazy and are less intelligent than those who are more affluent.

> Stereotype 2: People in poverty are lazy and have a weak work ethic.

"There is a common misconception... that low-income families are 'takers' who do not work, instead relying on government assistance to meet their needs" (Roberts, Povich, & Mather, 2013, p. 3). Such stereotypes of the "lazy welfare user" assume poverty is the result of defects in the moral character of individuals rather than structural barriers to opportunity (see Chapter 2). Arguing that we need a new paradigm for poverty, Mark Rank (2006) suggests that the new paradigm begin with a "recognition that American poverty is largely the result of structural, rather than individual, failings... [specifically], the inability of the economic, political, and social structures to provide the support and opportunities necessary to lift all Americans out of poverty" (p. 26).

A recent report from the U. S. Bureau of Labor Statistics (2014) outlines three major labor-market, poverty-related problems: low earnings/wages, periods of unemployment, and involuntary part-time employment, with the most significant problem being low wages. In the 1960s, the minimum wage kept a family of three

out of poverty (Cooper, 2013). Wages have been stagnant for a decade, and 4.4 million people work full-time but fail to lift their families out of poverty (U. S. Bureau of Labor Statistics, 2014). Even with full-time employment, minimum wage jobs do not pay enough to cover basic household expenses. "In no state, metropolitan area, or county can a full-time worker earning the prevailing minimum wage afford a modest two-bedroom apartment" (Yentel, 2016, p. 1). In 2016, to rent such an apartment, spending no more than a third of one's income on housing costs, required a worker to make at least $20.30 per hour, a wage that is far greater than the federal minimum wage of $7.25.

The availability of full-time jobs poses another problem. Many low-wage workers involuntarily work part-time or are employed in a series of temporary jobs between which they may experience periods of unemployment. Some employers intentionally provide only part-time work to avoid providing benefits mandated by full-time employment.

Our point is, laziness or a poor work ethic in those who live in poverty is not the problem. In fact, most people in poverty who are able and eligible to work do so. Of people living in poverty, 35 percent are not eligible to work because they are retired, disabled, or are students, and of the 65 percent eligible to work, 63 percent are working full- or part-time.

> Stereotype 3: People who live in poverty are not as smart as those who do not live in poverty.

In debunking this stereotype, we very briefly touch on findings from three fields of study: (1) hereditarianism, (2) intelligence testing, and (3) neuroscience. At the heart of this stereotype is the nature-versus-nurture debate. There are no legitimate studies, of which we are aware, that demonstrate people who live in poverty are inherently less intelligent than people who do not live in poverty.

In *Dismantling Contemporary Deficit Thinking*, Valencia (2010) documents the "pseudo-science" known as hereditarianism which has contributed to this stereotype. Hereditarianism is "the doctrine that genetics primarily accounts for individual differences in the behavior of human beings, as well as differences between groups" (p. 19). Valencia details the lack of scientific integrity in each of these studies and the resulting faulty conclusions. He unequivocally states there is no evidence to support the claim of inferior intelligence in people who live in poverty (2010).

Increasingly neuroscience is shedding light on the relationship between poverty and intelligence. Studies from this field have found that dealing with the "constant and all-consuming" adverse effects of poverty can render a person less able to focus on avenues that could lead out of poverty, such as education and job training. These stressors can also have an adverse impact on test performance. When people are preoccupied with the reality of living with severely limited financial resources, the impairment of their cognitive functioning compares to a 13-point drop in I.Q. (Mani, Mullainathan, Shafir, & Zhao, 2013).

Not only has the stress and strain of living in poverty been found to impair a person's cognitive functioning, living in poverty may also adversely affect brain structure. A team of neuroscientists led by Kimberly Noble and Elizabeth Sowell studied the association between socioeconomic status and children's brain structure (Noble et al., 2015). They conducted brain imaging on 1,099 children, adolescents, and young adults from low-income families and found that the surface area of the brain was smaller than the surface area in their wealthier peers. Yet, rather than drawing the conclusion that people are in poverty because the surface area of their brain is smaller, the researchers stressed their findings have implications for poverty-reduction policy, as their study demonstrated that an increase of a few thousand dollars in income and as little as one additional year of education were associated with significant increases in the surface area of the brain.

Lending credence to the idea that low intelligence does not cause poverty, Elliot Tucker-Drob and Timothy Bates (2016) conducted a meta-analysis that led them to conclude that living in poverty in the United States had a depressing effect on a person's developing intellect; however, such was not the case in the other participating countries. Data from 14 independent studies concluded living in poverty in the United States diminishes a person's ability to develop intellectual potential. In contrast, because the diminishing effect was not found in the other countries, researchers hypothesized that differences in access to educational opportunities, medical services, and income support provided through safety nets in the other countries may contribute to the difference between countries.

Studies such as these illustrate that low intelligence does not cause poverty; rather, adverse poverty-related factors can contribute to a dampening of intellectual potential. Additionally, they clearly point to the importance of anti-poverty interventions that counteract structural barriers found in institutions and the broader society. Too often, as educators we conclude that people who live in poverty are the problem. To create poverty-disrupting classrooms, we need to see *poverty as the problem* and *people as endowed with potential*.

VOICES FROM POVERTY

CELIA

I wanted to go into public health. When I graduated with a science degree, I had to do an internship with the county health department. I went to different schools to do lessons on topics such as tobacco awareness, dental health, nutrition, etc. I did that with 4th and 5th grade classes, and it was like magic when I got in there. The kids were paying attention and asking lots of thoughtful questions. I instantly fell in love with classroom teaching. It was never on my radar. Honestly, I was a horrible student and probably one of the most talkative kids. It wasn't something that I thought I'd ever do. I started teaching in '96; I've been teaching 20 years.

I grew up in the inner city. My parents didn't speak the language; they didn't understand how to access schooling and the system. They were just on survival mode most of the time.

My father was the single income earner, so most of the time we got help from the local church. I remember our priest would bring us bags of food and clothes. I didn't think anything of it; I just thought that most people got this stuff. Then as I got older, I realized we were poor. We shopped at the thrift store. We didn't go to the Macy's. There were six of us.

We got by, but as I got older, I realized that I didn't necessarily have the name-brand clothes that everyone else had. My brothers and I shared clothes. I remember wearing my uncle's jeans. I was in 7th grade and he was a grown man, so I had to roll the cuffs up four times and wear a belt because clearly his pants were too big for me.

I wasn't the best student in elementary school. I used to get in trouble. I talked too much. I wasn't on task. I required reteaching and I just remember some teachers being frustrated with me.

In junior high, I didn't know how to navigate the mix of cultures very well, so I just mimicked my friends and wanted to be a part of who they were. We moved two different times. In high school, we lived in an area where there was a lot of drug dealing and gang activity.

There was a gang that sold drugs directly in front of our house and two houses down, on the corner.

If they knew something was going to happen—they were fighting with another group or they felt like something was about to go down—they'd tell us, "Hey, you guys might want to lay low today. Don't hang out in the front. You might want to sleep on the floor." So we'd go, "OK, thanks for the information." So as a teacher, I have an urgency in me. Everything to me is life or death because we have students who live in areas that we know are gang-related.

I remember going to college and realizing how much I didn't know and how unprepared I was. I spent a whole year in remedial courses. That's when I realized that I had gotten a poor education, and that's always fueled my passion for what I do.

I feel that urgency when I'm in the classroom and in anything I do. I don't see it as I'm just teaching math. I see it as I'm giving you a skill to get you out of your circumstance. That's what I'm always thinking. I can't spare a minute. I can't waste any more time. Every minute counts. I could literally save someone's life. I really think that. It's not just, well, let me teach you how to write an essay. I have to teach you how to write so you can express yourself and you can pass your college-entrance writing test or apply for a job or write a grant or apply for a scholarship. I see it all as the steps down the road.

That's why I'm so big on teaching my kids to advocate for themselves. That's always the very first word I teach, the day-one vocabulary word: *advocate*. When I get students who are very shy and don't speak up, my mission with them is, by the time they leave me, they have to be able to stand up and participate in academic discourse because it's vital to their survival. So many times, I felt like I couldn't—I either didn't have the words or the courage or whatever it may be. I felt for so long I didn't have a voice. My job is to make sure that my kids know how to engage in society in a meaningful way, using their voice, using their thoughts. I would just say I have an urgency about teaching because I think about them 10 years, 15 years from now. ■

5 | DISRUPTION 3: COMMITTING TO EQUITY

I remember a student, my sweet Jesslyn. The first time she came into my classroom she propped her feet up on the desk. I remember thinking, "You have no clue who you're messing with right now." I told her, "You're going to learn, and you're going to follow instructions and do what's needed in order to excel in this class." We butted heads for a while. Actually a few times in the following weeks I had to talk with her outside the classroom, but I didn't let down. I had high expectations for her. Then she began to come in and talk to me. She told me how she had been doing drugs since she was like 11. She had pretty much tried everything. Her dad was in jail. Mom was too, off and on. She kind of lived here and there. In my mind, I was thinking this is like my brother who threw his life away for drugs. He went to prison. I remember telling her, "We're all going to fail miserably sometimes, but what we do when we get back on our feet is our choice. What's important is how we choose to regroup after our mistakes." She ended up dropping out of school.

I think the school kind of pushed her out. I was willing to bend over backwards and do whatever I needed to do. Was it unfair that I expected everybody else to do the same thing? Was it unfair that I expected all of the other five teachers she had to bend over backwards for her, and the administration too? Toward the end of this year I got a letter from her. She was in jail. I get that there are a lot of negative influences outside of school, but I really feel like she was somebody we let slip through the cracks. She was smart. She was capable. We just needed to level the playing field for her. It's interesting—when we realized our kids needed extra help with the new math standards, we quickly added an extra period to the day, which included a seminar for the struggling students. Why don't we do that for the students who need advocacy and a caring relationship? Why don't we create extra time for people who need a mental health break?

—*Nina, High School Teacher*

ANSWERING THE "WHO" QUESTION:
A 100-Word Reflection

From your perspective, what is the difference between "equitable" and "equal"? _____

_____

_____

_____

_____

_____

ANSWERING THE "WHAT" QUESTION:
WHAT THE RESEARCH TELLS US

Committing to Equity

Our society historically has placed great hope in public schooling as the great equalizer, and central to the American Dream. In his essay entitled "Saving Horatio Alger: Equality, Opportunity, and the American Dream," Richard Reeves (2014) explains,

> From its very beginnings the U.S. was unsurpassed among nations in its zeal for education... [T]he Founders were passionately committed to schooling, one of the great engines of social and economic advancement... As early as 1850, two-thirds of American children between five and 14 were in school (two-thirds of *white* children, it should be said), while back in England and Wales the proportion was only half. (p. 6)

Public schools have repeatedly been called upon to respond to demographic and societal changes since the inception of universal education. Figure 5.1 illustrates this connection. In the early 19th century, access to education was the goal. After World War II, schools were increasingly asked to move beyond mere access to ensuring equal opportunity, and in the later part of the 20th century, the call became one of higher outcomes for all students.

FIGURE 5.1 | U. S. Public Schooling's Historical Role as "The Great Equalizer"

Access to education for some	1837	Universal education through the elementary grades
	1896	Plessy v. Ferguson—U.S. Supreme Court decision validating the separation of black and white students and establishing the "separate but equal" doctrine
Equal educational opportunity for all	1954	Brown v. Topeka Board of Education—U.S. Supreme Court decision mandating the desegregation of schools
	1965	Elementary and Secondary Education Act (ESEA)—Part of the War on Poverty and authorizing federal funding for "disadvantaged students"
	1972	Title IX—Ensured equal opportunity based on gender
	1975	Education of All Handicapped Children Act (P.L. 94-142)
High achievement for all	1983	*A Nation at Risk: The Imperative for Educational Reform*—report by Ronald Reagan's National Commission on Excellence in Education
	1994	Goals 2000: Educate America Act (PL 103-227)
	2002	Reauthorization of ESEA as No Child Left Behind
	2015	Reauthorization of ESEA as Every Student Succeeds Act

Three Compatible Goals

In *Turning High-Poverty Schools into High-Performing Schools* (Parrett & Budge, 2012), we described how leaders in the schools we studied strove for three ideals—excellence, equality, and equity. We explained how these leaders understood the meaning of the ideals and the possible tension between the three. Excellence was not sacrificed in the service of the other two ideals. Curriculum was not watered down; standards were not lowered. All students were expected and supported to meet high standards. It was through equitable distribution of resources (time, people, money) that these schools leveled the playing field and made access to opportunity more equal.

Teachers we interviewed for this book understood these three ideals as well. They maintained high expectations for their students and supported them in meeting those expectations largely by committing to equity in their classrooms. They understood that treating all students the same, although it sounds fair and just, is actually unfair and unjust. By providing the support students needed, even if some required more support than others, they were ensuring all students had a level playing field from which to reach the high expectations they held for them.

In his book *Rac(e)ing to Class: Confronting Poverty and Race in Schools and Classrooms,* Richard Milner (2015) uses the term "school dependent" to describe those students for whom equity and leveling the playing field are often essential to their success. "Being school dependent can mean students rely on school for basic needs such as breakfast and lunch, nutritious snacks, and academic support, as well as exposure to museums and other learning centers outside the traditional classroom" (p. 49).

Inequality and Inequity: What Is the Difference?

Before we go too much further, we want to clarify how we will be using two terms: *inequality* and *inequity*. *Inequality* is quantitative in nature and refers to conditions being unequal. *Inequity* refers to a qualitative dimension. Synonyms for inequity are *injustice* and *unfairness*. For example, we could say inequality in student outcomes result, at least in part, from inequity in school systems.

Nothing Easy About It

Committing to equity requires educators to gain two kinds of clarity: ontological clarity (understanding "who one is" and how one wants "to be" in the world) and ideological clarity about their role as a teacher. Understanding that teaching is a political rather than a neutral act (Cooper, 2003), we come to realize that there is nothing easy about making a commitment to equity. The teachers we interviewed had to do their own reflection and soul-searching to confront their mental maps about poverty, student responsibility, parental responsibility, fairness, and justice. They often experimented with different approaches to such practices as grading, assessment, and homework before landing on those they felt were congruent with their commitments and values.

Nina, Jesslyn's teacher in the introductory scenario, was frustrated by the inequity in the system and what she viewed as an unwillingness of other teachers and administrators to level the playing field for Jesslyn. Her questions were not rhetorical; they were earnest. Other teachers we talked to, including those, like Nina, who grew up in poverty, struggled with notions of fairness and justice. Although many were able to recognize the ways school or district policies, processes, or structures disadvantaged some groups of students and privileged others, when asked to describe their equity-oriented actions, they primarily stayed within the confines of their own classroom. They tended not to think in terms of groups (e.g., their students who lived in poverty as a group in contrast to those who did not live in poverty); rather, they individualized and personalized their equity-oriented action.

Three Research-Based Approaches to Equity-Oriented Professional Practice

In what follows we highlight three different conceptualizations for equity-oriented professional practice: cultural proficiency, equity literacy, and anti-bias education. As you continue reading, we urge you to consider the similarities among them, as well as their congruency with what we have suggested in this book is needed to disrupt poverty's adverse influence on learning.

Cultural Proficiency

In their book *Culturally Proficient Education: An Asset-Based Response to Conditions of Poverty,* the authors assert that gaining cultural proficiency requires a paradigm shift from "tolerating children of poverty" [to] "transformational commitment to equity without regard to students' social class" (Lindsey, Karns, & Myatt, 2010, p. 53). They illustrate the shift as a developmental process that is about "who we are, more than what we do...," predicated on a person's ability and willingness to view the change needed as an "inside out" process (p. 52).

Equity Literacy

Viewing cultural proficiency as only part of the skill set needed to address diverse groups of learners, Paul Gorski and his colleague Katy

Swalwell chose the term "equity literacy" to center discussions about diversity in education on "equity and justice" rather than culture. Gorski (2013) defines equity literacy as "the skills and dispositions that enable us to recognize, respond to, and redress conditions that deny some students access to the educational opportunities enjoyed by their peers and, in doing so, sustain equitable learning environments for all students and families" (p. 19). In addition to drawing from cultural proficiency theory, Gorski and Swalwell's construct of equity literacy is informed by resiliency theory and a concept known as "funds of knowledge"—knowledge that is historically accumulated and culturally developed, which is vital to individual, family, and community well-being (Moll, Amanti, Neff, & Gonzalez, 1992).

Anti-Bias Education

Beverly Daniel Tatum, scholar, educator, and former president of Spelman College says, "We absorb bias in the same way we breathe in smog—involuntarily and usually without any awareness of it" (as cited in Fiarman, 2016, p. 10). Anti-bias education in general is designed to support respect for diversity and embracing differences, as well as recognizing and acting against bias and injustice. To learn more about anti-bias programs and activities being implemented in schools across the country, check out Teaching Tolerance, a project of the Southern Poverty Law Center that serves as a clearinghouse of information. Educators and others interested can find many resources for furthering their equity-oriented work at www.teachingtolerance.org.

At the core of each of these approaches, as well as our own, is the importance of answering the "who" question—who am I? What do I believe? What are my blind spots and biases? How do I become more aware of my tacitly held mental maps? Each of these conceptualizations also attempts to get at the "what" question, as they are founded on a set of values, principles, or tenets. And, they tackle the "how" question, calling for specific sets of skills or competencies to be employed in the service of creating more equitable and just learning environments for all students. "The challenge for schools in the 21st century is the extent to which we embrace the mandate to educate all children and youth. To do so requires soul-searching on the part of our schools and those of us who are the educators within those schools" (Lindsey, Karns, & Myatt, 2010, p. 37).

A Litmus Test for Equity in the Classroom: Three Key Practices

Although efforts to confront inequity most efficiently occur at the systemic level, individual educators can successfully take on inequity as well. Three practices that can be "hot button" issues for teachers, interestingly, are also a good litmus test for a person's orientation toward equity—homework, grading, and classroom-based assessment. In what follows, we have combined advice from those we interviewed with what we know about developing equity-centered, effective practice.

Homework

Despite its abundance, the research on the effectiveness of homework is inconclusive (Hattie, 2009; Vatterott, 2009). Some of the teachers we interviewed assign homework to their students, while others do not. For students who live in poverty, homework can present many challenges, including parents being unavailable for support; no quiet space in which to work; lack of educational resources and supplies; and lack of equipment such as computers, mobile devices, and connectivity to high-speed Internet—or even electricity. Time to complete homework can also be compromised as students who live in poverty may have responsibility for their siblings, cooking or other household chores, and part-time jobs needed to support their families.

These students may be reluctant to share with teachers the circumstances under which they struggle to complete homework assignments. A recent study found nearly 50 percent of students reported they were unable to complete homework assignments due to lack of a computer or Internet access, and 42 percent said they received a lower grade on an assignment because they did not have access to the Internet (Hispanic Heritage Foundation, 2015). Etta Kralovec (2000), coauthor of *The End of Homework: How Homework Disrupts Families, Overburdens Children, and Limits Learning,* listed inability to complete homework among students' top reasons for dropping out of high school.

David, a 5th grade teacher, told us he had become more thoughtful about assigning homework. He explained,

> The first time I took a long, hard examination of my homework practice was after I had Mary in class. She was homeless and living in a car. I wasn't

supposed to know that, but she told me. They had to move around a lot. She'd tell me, "The security guard tapped on the glass and we had to move the car to a place where there was not light."

On the other hand, Alex, who teaches middle school asserted,

I assign homework. Everyone says that low-income kids can't do homework—at least, that is what I've heard; but this year I had an insanely successful experience with homework. I am talking about pretty much every kid did his or her homework every week. I made the homework meaningful. It went along with what I taught, and it wasn't fluff. It was specifically related to what applied to the standard, which applied specifically toward the upcoming test. I also gave them a sticker they could collect and use in exchange for granola bars or fruit snacks. I assigned homework on Mondays and it was due on Thursdays. If it wasn't turned in on Thursday, they were in with me at lunch. I would usually have fewer than 10 kids out of 120.

Anna, who teaches 1st grade, told us she provides all the necessary materials for students to complete their homework.

My whole room is superhero-themed. Every student has a hero binder. I gave them to the kids at the beginning of the year. I stress how important it is to be responsible for something. They are supposed to bring it back to school every day. I put everything they need to do their homework in the binder, and I send a book home each day from the classroom library. The kids have been phenomenal. I don't think I've had any of them lose it.

Those who have studied homework say it should be purposeful and well thought out (Neason, 2017). Cathy Vatterott (2009), author of *Rethinking Homework: Best Practices That Support Diverse Needs,* suggests homework be used for practice or to check for understanding. Homework should not be graded, she asserts. For students who lack the resources or support to complete homework, losing points or recess can be counterproductive. "We are basically punishing them for their poverty" (Vatterott, as cited in Neason, 2017, p. 5). Given the equity implications, as educators we should revisit our homework practices, and if we determine that homework is necessary (believing it improves student learning), then it is incumbent upon us to ensure all students have an equal opportunity to complete the homework. Anything less is an injustice.

Grading

Doug Reeves (2008) calls grading "the last frontier of teacher discretion" and asserts that if teachers want to improve their failure rate, they need to look no further than revamping their grading practices. Joe Feldman (2015), a national authority on grading, agrees with Reeves. In his blog entitled *How Grading Supports Inequity and What We Can Do About It*, Feldman calls improving grading an "incredibly powerful lever for strengthening equity in every element of teaching" and notes that grading is typically "not open for discussion." Nonetheless, opening the discussion, if only with one's self, can be a critical step toward making a commitment to equity.

Teachers interviewed for this book had gained a storehouse of wisdom that often began with taking a hard look at homework and other practices that informed their grading systems. Anton shared the following:

> I've been to two PD classes on grading, as I am trying to get ahead of the curve for the new school board policy that will start next year. In a nutshell, the "zero" grade is obsolete on the 100-point scale, since mathematically it is purely punitive. I also have eliminated any penalty for late work. If my job is to evaluate the degree to which the student accomplished the targeted standard, it doesn't make any sense for me to take an arbitrary 5 or 10 percent off due to the work being late. As a parent, I want to look at my child's grade and see the percentage to which the standard was accomplished.
>
> I communicate to all parents that I will always flag the assignment as late, but never take points; I will grade it at face value. I tell the parents that until the standards include the phrase "the student will be able to (fill in the blank) on time," I have no business assessing the timeliness. I pay attention to patterns. Once a student has three late flags, I contact parents and just talk to them, in a nonjudgmental or punitive way, and say, "Look, I'm seeing a pattern and it may hurt this student in a real-world application." Quite frequently, parents will agree to a change in policy that says their kid may not submit the work late for a certain amount of time to set a new pattern. It works so much better when it comes from the parent.
>
> I have had almost a full year now with the new grading policy, and like just about everything in this profession, the most equitable grading policy stems from knowing each student very well, building and maintaining a solid relationship, and communicating actively with home and counselors.

We have decades of research on grading practices and know what constitutes best practice (Brookhart, 2009; Cizek, 2010; Guskey & Bailey, 2001;

Marzano, 2000; McMillan, 2001); yet, such practices are rarely employed (Reeves, 2016). Effective grading practices provide accurate, timely, and specific feedback (Reeves, 2008). Poor grading practices can be at best ineffective, and at worst, inequitable. Figure 5.2 outlines five ineffective and inequitable grading practices.

FIGURE 5.2 | Ineffective and Inequitable Grading Practices

Practice	Problem
Using zeros for missing work and averaging scores	The use of zeros results in a mathematical flaw on a 100-point scale (Reeves, 2004).
Weighting all work in a grading period the same and averaging scores	Grades should represent the learning process. Assigning the same weight to both formative and summative assessments and averaging scores is a questionable practice in terms of accurately reflecting the learning process or the degree to which a student has gained mastery of the standard.
Deducting "points" for misbehavior	Ninety years of research demonstrates that the use of grades as punishment does not work (Guskey, 2000).
Basing a grade on a single assessment	It is questionable that any kind of single measure is an accurate reflection of "mastery."
Conflating academic learning with other dimensions of learning (e.g., social-emotional factors, behavior, work habits)	Grades should reflect a single dimension of learning. Conflating academic learning with social-emotional factors or behavior "muddies the water," at best, and at worst, is unjust.

Conflating academic learning with other dimensions of learning is a practice we see all too frequently, as in the vignette about Mr. Johnstone and Mr. Walther at the beginning of Chapter 1. Teachers too often conflate a variety of factors when assigning grades—late assignments, incomplete homework, retest penalties, attendance, behavior, work habits, and extra credit—to name a few. This practice is ineffective and inequitable. Such a grade does not accurately or specifically communicate what a student knows and is able to do in terms of the academic learning the grade is intended to represent. As Joe Feldman (2015) explains,

> [When] a grade is a composite of so many disparate elements it becomes impossible to understand what the grade represents. What does a "B" describe? That a student mastered the academic content, but came late every day? That the student understood only some of the standards, but completed all assignments on time (even if incorrect), and was kind to classmates? That the student aced major assessments, but was disrespectful? If a single grade can represent entirely different student profiles, then it provides no guidance to an individual student or her caregivers about her achievement or what she needs to improve. *There are few things more inequitable than hiding the path to success* (emphasis added).

Jon, one of the teachers we interviewed, echoed Feldman's sentiments when he told us,

> Student behavior has nothing to do with my grade book. For example, for a student earning a B+ in English, [the grade] should only speak to the student's ability to meet English standards. In other words, when someone looks at a student's B+ on the transcript, that someone should not have to wonder how much of that grade is weighted with behavior or participation assessments/points.

Students who live in poverty may be particularly disadvantaged when teachers conflate academic learning with other dimensions. For instance, the students may come from homes that are not conducive to completing homework, may have greater behavioral challenges, or are experiencing trauma. Moreover, many of the factors typically conflated with academics are based entirely on teachers' subjective judgment. Given what we know about the importance of our mental maps and the influence of bias and stereotypes, coupled with what we learned in Chapter 4 about teacher expectations, conflating academics with other dimensions of learning can result in inequities.

Students and their families need feedback on social-emotional and behavioral learning, but those dimensions should be assessed and graded separately. Lissa Pijanowski's (2011) article "The Case of the Illogical Grades" documents one district's journey toward improved grading practices, and it includes a rubric for assessing students' work habits. Likewise,

Andrew Miller's 2016 post on Edutopia provides several ideas for making grading practices more effective and equitable. He suggests resources for addressing behavioral issues, test retakes, "redoing" assignments, and test reflection intended to get students thinking about their strengths and areas for growth, as well as their study habits.

Classroom-Based Assessment

One of the greatest concerns related to equity and classroom-based assessment is simply recognizing the far reaching consequences our assessment practices can have on students. Teachers we interviewed described various ways in which they strive to make their classroom assessment practices equitable, such as allowing students to retake tests, providing targeted tutoring, offering students multiple options for demonstrating what they know and can do, requiring "practice" tests for those who need them, and asking students to reflect on their performance, as well as their preparation for the test.

Although teachers are constrained by school schedules, testing windows, and grading periods, to the degree possible, teachers who disrupt poverty make "time" the variable rather than "learning." In other words, within the system-imposed constraints they face, the goal is to allow students to work to mastery through multiple attempts to demonstrate what they know and can do. Several teachers said they allow students to retake tests, redo assignments, and refine projects. Anton explained,

> All students may retest, based on an authentic effort on the original. I ask students to make application to retest, where they have to assemble evidence of what they did to learn the material before they can retest. That works really well at the start of the year, but by the time I know the kids, it's not necessary. I can see the patterns, and an honest conversation saves time and paperwork.

Consider using the 10 questions in Figure 5.3 to support your efforts to use equitable assessment practices.

Educators who disrupt poverty disrupt inequity. They level the playing field for students in poverty and are willing to rethink their practices to ensure they are fair and just for all students. In what follows, we offer five practical suggestions gleaned from the teachers we interviewed for creating equitable classrooms.

FIGURE 5.3 | Equitable Classroom-Based Assessment: 10 Questions to Ask

1. Have I clearly communicated (via a rubric or other means) what I am expecting students to know and do?

2. Do I use multiple measures and multiple kinds of measures?

3. Do I teach test-taking skills to those students who need such instruction, or offer practice tests?

4. Do I compare students against the standard rather than to other students?

5. Do I provide flexibility, when possible, in the time required for performance?

6. Can students choose from self-selected or teacher-selected assessment items?

7. Am I sure the assessments I use are free of cultural- or class-based bias?

8. Do I challenge my interpretation of student work through dialogue with colleagues or other means?

9. Do I conference with students about their assessments, asking them to reflect on strengths, weaknesses, study habits, and preparation?

10. Do I allow retakes?

ANSWERING THE "HOW" QUESTION:
Tips from Teachers

Five Practical Suggestions for Committing to Equity in the Classroom

As you read through the teachers' suggestions, you will hear echoes of poverty-disrupting ideas presented in past chapters. Understanding the adverse effects of poverty, building caring relationships, and holding high expectations are closely linked to the considerations we make when we commit to equity.

1. Know What Your Students Need

When we queried teachers about equity, it was no surprise to hear them return to the importance of relationships and knowing your students well. Many attributed their ability to "meet their students where they were" to the caring relationships they had established with them. Leslie described a conversation she had with her 1st graders about "everyone getting what they need" and the fact that one of their classmates would be following "a different set of rules" that would help him to be successful. She remembered the other students being accepting and supportive of the personalized arrangement made for one of their classmates.

Jon described how he worked to establish consistency and a nonjudgmental climate over time to enable a student who had previously struggled in other contexts to flourish. He explained,

> There was a student, Leo. He couldn't pronounce his *R*s and *L*s very well. He was kind of a bigger kid and had a really bad temper. He was known for walking out of classrooms and cussing out the teachers and other students. I had him for three years. Leo was "Below Basic" consistently in all subjects on his state tests. After the first year I had him, he scored "Advanced" in all but one area, on which he was "Proficient." I'd like to say it was because I am an amazing teacher and know my content so well, but it's because I knew Leo so well. We had a wonderful relationship.

Some teachers spoke of something we call "keeping your eye on the prize." They refrained from getting into power struggles with their students over lost binders, chewed up pencils, and "forgotten" supplies. Such power struggles deflected from the learning that needed to occur, and for the most part, they had established routines and structures that turned such issues into nonissues. The focus remained on student learning instead of whether or not a student needed to be "more responsible." As Miranda put it,

> Kids are kids. They don't understand their emotions, so their first response is to shut down. You have to figure out why. Did he have breakfast? Does he have his supplies? Does he have a pencil? I don't ask, "What did you do with the pencil I gave you last August?" I have a bucket of pencils. You have to understand what is not working for each kid and fix it.

2. Meet Basic Needs to Clear the Way for Learning

In high-poverty/high-performing schools, we witnessed numerous examples of educators collectively responding to the basic needs of their students—from providing breakfast, lunch, and sometimes dinner, to offering clothing boutiques, engaging in partnerships with food banks, and sending home backpacks filled with food for the weekend. Like so many educators, the teachers we interviewed often did what they could individually too. They spoke of trying to meet students' basic needs by keeping food, clothing, and basic hygiene supplies in their rooms. James described his approach, saying,

> I understand we can't influence some things. But there are some things that we can, so why not do those things. Don't expect someone else to do it. Sometimes conversations with kids are hard. Let's be honest. It's not an easy conversation to have with a junior-high-age kid about things like hygiene. I talk to them about it in a kind way and provide them with an opportunity to do something. We give them resources—a shower maybe, a clean set of clothes, some deodorant,... I keep gel in my room. I'll be like, "Hey, I've got some gel here." They go into the bathroom and fix their hair. We do these things and then just move on. It's not something we need to focus on, just do what we can to help them out.

3. Differentiate, Scaffold, Model—but Don't "Dumb Down"!

Maintaining high standards for all students was a frequently voiced value in ensuring an equitable classroom environment. Teachers had many suggestions for supporting students. Some described how they ensured equal participation through the use of equity sticks (often a set of popsicle sticks inscribed with students' names from which the teacher draws to randomly call on students) or spreadsheets for tracking student-teacher interactions. Celia explained her theory of action:

> Sometimes in classrooms, the kids who know the most or are not as afraid are the ones who always volunteer or get called on. And then those other quiet kids—it's easy to lose them in the shuffle in a class of 32 kids. So make sure you have the right systems in place, whether it be numbered heads or equity sticks or whatever system that ensures that every kid gets a chance to speak at least once every hour of the day. Making sure everybody gets a voice, gets a say, is important.

Others explained how they differentiated instruction, provided scaffolds in the form of models, and extended learning time. For example, Marissa delineated several ways she maintains high standards and supports her students:

> Prior to writing, we have debates. The kids really enjoy debating, and I feel like it helps them prepare to write. We read an article together and then

they can voice their opinions, taking turns, and going back to each other's arguments. Those students who really don't know where they stand, they get to hear what other students have to say. It helps them determine where they stand on an issue. I also do a lot of modeling. I do think-out-louds, and I show them steps. I also differentiate. I'll pull a small group, and I'll review vocabulary terms or will do some guided practice to prepare for the next day. I also use a lot of visuals and manipulatives.

Marissa is also very intentional about building a community of learners among students, which provides another source of support for students who need it. She continued,

One of the sections in our [literacy] rubric is questioning—the questions they ask one another. So I've been working a lot on prompting students. If they see their friend struggle, they have learned to ask him or her a question to help them get started. Just one question can trigger them. They'll ask a question like, "What is the numerator?" and they'll look at the chart on the wall. So asking each other questions is something that also helps them.

4. Help Students Become Advocates for Their Own Learning

Increasing students' investment in their own learning was another way teachers committed to equity. In many of the interviews, teachers relayed the importance they placed on empowering students, even young students, by helping them understand themselves as learners. Anton shared this advice:

It's just a lot of knowing your kids, using data, and then presenting it in a way to them that is honest and authentic. The "points thing" is what kills it. If you tell kids, "If you read at this level you get this many points," then the focus for those kids becomes the grade and there is never that moment of honesty that says, "Look, you read at a 5th grade level, and I care about you enough to address this. It doesn't mean that you are stupid; it just means that you have tremendous potential for growth in reading, but it starts with not being embarrassed, hiding, not behaving well in class, and just side-stepping the issue." I could go on forever about techniques, programs, policies; but the fundamental key is that the student must trust you, and the relationship is the singular key to growth. They are young, insecure; can you imagine being that age and a low-level reader? It is socially awkward enough being a teenager; now let's add in labels and grades—that's a real plan for failure. So build that relationship, put together some data, have an honest conversation, get rid of the "points and grade games" and deal with growth.

5. Advocate for Change

As we stated earlier, most teachers described their commitment to equity in terms of what they did in their own classrooms. A few, such as Nina, the teacher in the vignette at the beginning of this chapter, were spreading their wings and learning how to advocate for changes in their school.

David told us the story of a 1st grader who loved the pizza served occasionally for lunch. This young man would take note of the days pizza was going to be served and eagerly anticipated lunch on those days. One day David was in the lunchroom on a pizza day and the young man was in line. When he reached the serving area, the server said, "You don't have any punches left; you'll need to take a sack lunch" and pointed to a small table where brown bags contained a cheese sandwich and a carton of milk. Seeing the tears in the student's eyes, David asked the lunch server if an exception could be made. When she shrugged her shoulders, he went to speak to the kitchen supervisor, who explained it was district policy. She hated it too, but her hands were tied. David offered to pay for the student's lunch, and the supervisor said that would be a violation of policy also. He told us,

> I went to my principal and said, "What can we do about it?" And she said, "The parents have to learn at some point. At some point, you can't keep handing things out." And I just so whole-heartedly disagree with that, that you're going to teach the parents a lesson by depriving a 6-year-old. That's just so opposite of anything that I hold dear and believe.

David returned to his classroom, closed the door, and cried. As he explained, it wasn't about one student being denied a hot lunch for a day. For him, it was the "injustice" of the situation. The young man's parents had chosen to not apply for the free and reduced-price lunch program, although they would likely have qualified. It bothered him enough that he continued to advocate for change, but he was not successful. "How often do we punish students for things they can't control?" he asked.

Our discussion of equity—and of the other poverty-disrupting actions we have discussed—continues in the next chapter; however, for some additional specific suggestions for committing to equity, see Figure 5.4. Building relationships, holding high expectations, and providing the needed support to meet those expectations, together with committing to equity, all converge when we take responsibility for every student learning. We are reminded of the cartoon with two kids and a dog. One kid says to the other, "I taught Spot to whistle." When Spot doesn't whistle, the other kid says, "Hey, I thought you said you taught Spot to whistle," to which the first kid replies, "I said I taught him; I didn't say he learned it." If something isn't learned, has it been taught? What do you do when students do not learn? This question is central to the poverty-disrupting action we discuss next— holding ourselves professionally accountable for learning.

APPLYING YOUR LEARNING TO YOUR PRACTICE

- Think of a time when you benefited from being treated equitably instead of equally. What happened? How did it help you? How did it contribute to your mental map about fairness?
- What do you believe to be the difference between "leveling the playing field" and "dumbing down"?
- How are you "leveling the playing field" in your classroom? Why did you choose to level the playing field in this way? What difference is it making for students?

Application of Learning Matrix

To help you apply what you are learning to your professional practice, see Appendix A. Each chapter's high-leverage question is listed there, with space to list each student and reflect on what you know. Teachers with more than 25 students may want to use multiple matrices or select a particular class period. For this chapter, here is the high-leverage question: Is _____ [student's name] school dependent? If so, what does this student most need from school to level the playing field?

FIGURE 5.4 | Ideas for Committing to Equity in Homework, Grading, and Assessment

See Beyond Poverty—Focus on the strengths, assets, and cultural funds of knowledge students bring to the classroom.

Superhero Folders—Keeping in mind that all students do not have equal access to resources, one teacher sends home a weekly folder with all the supplies needed to complete homework and a book from the classroom library. She emphasizes returning the folder as the "responsibility" aspect of homework, but does not punish or lower grades if the folder is not returned. Her folder return rate is nearly 100 percent.

Use Rubrics to "See" the End in Mind—Provide access to rubrics before assignments so students can "see" your expectations ahead of time and use rubrics to provide formative feedback before grading.

Zero Use of Zero—The use of zeros results in a mathematical flaw on a 100-point scale. Abandon the use of zero in your grading practice. An excellent resource on the topic is available at http://www.tolerance.org/blog/zero-effect.

Fail Safe—Make failure safe and a key component of learning. Explicitly teach the concept that failure is a "normal" part of learning. Begin by providing students with opportunities that are "low risk" and ungraded, such as creating Rube Goldberg machines, building spaghetti/marshmallow towers, or using "breakout boxes"—stacking boxes with multiple "combination locks," each requiring a code to open, and in which a series of clues is provided to solve a problem. Follow these activities by debriefing the experience, and point to the many times failure led to new learning.

Reflect, Then Redo or Retest—Ask students to reflect on how they prepared for an assignment or a test. Help them plan for better preparation and allow them to redo the assignment or retake the test. *Fair Isn't Always Equal* by Rick Wormeli (2006) is a good resource for grading in a differentiated classroom.

Making *Time*, Not *Learning*, the Variable—Allow students to gain a feeling of control and agency over their own learning by teaching them that mastery is the primary goal, not rapid completion of an assignment. Provide extra time when possible for those who need it and support for students to reach their goals by encouraging revisions based on clear feedback.

Goal Setting—Engage students in setting academic goals, collecting data, and charting their progress.

Portfolios—Use portfolios to develop metacognition and assessment literacy in students.

Include the Kids—Involve students in setting criteria for assignments and projects. Begin by brainstorming the answer to the question: "What makes a good _____ [fill in the blank with the project or assignment]? Sort the brainstormed attributes into categories and create a T-chart. T-charts can later be developed into rubrics. *Setting and Using Criteria* by Gregory, Cameron, and Davies (2011) provides several examples of ways to involve students in developing criteria for assessing assignments or projects.

Challenging Our Mental Maps:
Learning, Unlearning, and Relearning Summary

Pause for a few minutes and use the following questions to consider your current thinking as it relates to the information and ideas presented in this chapter.

Learning: What conceptions did you hold about equity before reading this chapter?

Unlearning: How, if at all, did the chapter challenge your beliefs or thinking?

Relearning: How might this "challenge to your thinking" or new idea be beneficial or helpful to you?

Action: What *action* will you take, and why?

As you consider your answers and progress through this book, record your answers for each chapter in the summary table supplied in Appendix B. The summary table provides you with a model for exploring your mental map, reflecting on current practice, developing your theory of action, and planning next steps.

 ## COMMUNITIES OF PRACTICE:
Extending Your Learning with Others

- Discuss your understanding of the difference between *equal* and *equitable*.
- How have we explored the gaps that exist in our school related to poverty and achievement?
- In our school, which is the variable—learning or time? What is our evidence?
- Discuss the idea of providing students with multiple opportunities to pass exams without adversely affecting grades.
- Does our school provide additional quality instructional time for learning? What are some examples?
- In our school, do *all* students have access to the materials, equipment, space, and time to complete assignments (including homework)? How do we know this?

- What resources are available in our school, district, and community to support our efforts to better understand and confront inequities our students face at school and home?

Challenging Stereotypes to Commit to Equity

> *Stereotype 4: Education as a way out of poverty is readily available to all.*

Although public schooling has made significant strides toward the three ideals of excellence, equality, and equity, significant injustices still remain. An examination of some of these inequities challenges the fourth stereotype. This stereotype is deeply engrained in the American psyche and is akin to the "bootstrap" notion that anyone can rise above their circumstances if they work hard enough. The logic behind the myth goes something like this: education is the means to upward mobility, and public schooling is free and readily available to everyone; thus, anyone with enough fortitude, hard work, and personal responsibility can pull themselves up from poverty by availing themselves of an education. Yet, as Lindsey, Karns, and Myatt (2010) charge, "Our schools, like the society in which they are nested ... reflect systemic inequities. They have from the beginning of our country" (p. 31). Such systemic inequities illuminate the problem with the bootstrap logic. Let's take a look at what we mean.

Broad Systemic Inequity

A person's zip code continues to determine, in large part, the quality of the education that a person receives in the United States. Reeves (2014) asserts, "[A]fter decades of rhetoric and reform, the American education system is failing as an engine of social mobility. The poorest children (Black and White alike) receive the worst public education. Achievement gaps between poor and affluent children tend to widen, rather than narrow, during the K–12 years" (p. 16). Indeed, the long history of inequitable treatment of students of color and those from low-income families has been well documented (Banks, 1997; Brown, Benkovitz, Mutillo, & Urban, 2011; Delpit, 1995; Ladson-Billings, 1994, 2009; Larson & Ovando, 2001; Rist, 1979; Valenzuela, 1999).

"Savage inequalities," as Jonathan Kozol (1991) in his award-winning best seller of the same title named them, exist between the quality of schooling provided to students who live in poverty and students of color in contrast to their white and more affluent counterparts. Such inequalities can be found in several facets of the system, including teacher quality (Linda Darling-Hammond, 2010; Goldhaber, Lavery, & Theobald, 2015); school facilities (Kozol, 1991); and learning time (Desimone & Long, 2010; Rogers & Mirra, 2014). To elaborate, high-poverty schools tend to have teachers who are less experienced and teaching outside their certification, as well as school buildings in disrepair and limited infrastructure to support technology. Additionally, poverty-related issues, including welcoming a constant stream of new students (high rates of mobility), school lockdowns, teacher absences, and inefficient transitions from class to class, can result in less learning time in high-poverty schools (Rogers & Mirra, 2014).

Inequity at the District and School-System Level

Leslie, one of the teachers we interviewed, conveyed her "aha" moment in coming to understand firsthand the inequality that exists in school districts. She shared her experience:

> We went on four or five field trips in the semester I was at Howard Elementary. We had eight or nine parents every time. We had tons of parents to help out; they paid for everything. Everything was taken care of. When I went to Jackson Elementary, we took one field trip during the whole

year—to the zoo. I had only one parent volunteer, who had to get permission from the principal and his parole officer to help out.

Leslie's experience is not uncommon. Among schools within the same district, it is not unusual to find great inequality in terms of, for example, personnel, school facilities, and parental volunteers. Additionally, in both districts and schools, students of color and students in poverty are often overrepresented in special education and remedial programs; underrepresented in advanced course work, gifted and talented programs, and extracurricular activities; and disproportionally represented in disciplinary infractions. Rigid ability grouping, tracking, and retention are common practices that too often result in unequal access to deep learning for students in poverty.

VOICES FROM POVERTY

My parents were 19. I was born in a big city; they were up there for school, but that didn't last. We literally stayed for about nine days after I was born, born at the end of the '60s to a couple of hippy teenagers. They decided to move back in with my grandmother on my dad's side. This was a very strong, Southern-raised, African American woman. Rules were fairly clear for me, at least growing up.

When I became school age, that's where I would go after school so my parents could pick me up. That was a critical piece. My grandpa was an old-school guy. The Golden Rule and respect and work hard. I don't know how many lectures I heard when I was a kid about "no one can take your education away from you." My grandmother had actually left the South as a kid to move up north to live with her aunt and uncle so she wouldn't have to go to segregated schools. So she made real sure that I understood the value of having an equal opportunity at school.

I was a mixed kid—dad's black, mom's white. Mom's side of the family is Jewish, so I spent time at temple one day at the beginning of the weekend and I'd be at a gospel church on Sunday. It was a rich experience, and it made me very aware of the differences. I was too light-skinned when I was with my dad's side of the family, and when I was with mom's side I was too dark. So there were a lot of remarks and jokes and questions about having curly hair.

My parents were starting to get a little more established workwise. Mom was a nurse; dad was a manager at a furniture place. But L.A. just started getting crazy, so they wanted a different place to live. We loaded up a '77 Volkswagen van and literally drove around the U.S. one summer, ending up in the Northwest. We camped outside of a coastal town for a couple of days. My folks liked it, and the next year it was like this hippie caravan of my folks' friends heading north.

Boy, it was a culture shock coming from the inner city to rural, coastal America. Dirt road, the beach. I was 10. I didn't know how to ride a bike. In the city, you just walked everywhere.

Coming into school, it was very clear that my inner-city education did not have me ready. I wasn't reading at the same level; math was challenging. I had some great teachers early on; I also had a couple of terrible ones. That was my first awareness that the relationship piece was critical. One of my first teachers really kept me in line—didn't take any of my grief, had me work my butt off. Another one, an old white lady, didn't really care about me. I got in fights in her class; I got kicked out. I think I got suspended in 6th grade.

It was actually a male teacher across the way who basically removed me from her class. And for whatever reason, he saw something in me. I just remember starting to get into math. School started to become enjoyable. He seemed to really care. But I remember in the afternoons I'd go back to her class and I'd just screw off.

In middle school, I got into a couple of fights; there was a lot of racial tension. There were only three black kids in my whole middle school. Middle school was a trip for me.

I got into athletics, and then I had an art class that I really wasn't too into, but the teacher pulled me aside, gave me a camera; asked if I wanted to take pictures. So I got into that. The next thing I know, I became the senior photo editor for our newspaper. Our newspaper was the 11th-top high school newspaper in the nation, and it gave me that identity piece. I was good at this thing, so I stuck with sports and photography and had a 3.0.

Getting into our junior and senior years, everybody seemed like they were going to college. And I literally assumed that was the next thing to do. I don't remember talking about it with my parents at all, just my grandparents.

So I started applying to universities; I started getting in. I got a couple scholarships. I ended up at one of the smaller state universities and then actually flunked out halfway through my sophomore year. No idea what I was doing. No study skills, no study habits, no nothing; so I literally just bombed out.... My parents had split up when I was in high school. Mom moved back to California and then got a job out of state. So there was no family around. I was 19.

I lost my academic eligibility for a scholarship. That was probably my gut check that something had to change. I remember coming home at Christmas break, giving my mom the letter, seeing the look on her face. So I went to community college, got my associates degree, and with a different attitude graduated from another state college as a PE major with a psych and health minor.

I went into teaching. At this point, I was much more motivated. Even when I got back to college, I was taking 20 to 22 credits a semester. I was a man on a mission at that point.... I think some folks have to hit that rock bottom. I think it's a little easier to look back on, but at the time I wasn't really certain that I was going to pull it off. But it was good; I was much more focused, and getting a teaching job was pretty easy. That's where it started, and 20 years later, over a decade of being a teacher and now a principal, and I still love it! ■

6 DISRUPTION 4: ACCEPTING PROFESSIONAL ACCOUNTABILITY FOR LEARNING

Yeah, teachers get frustrated, and rightfully so... For the first few years in public school... I raised my voice. I yelled; I got frustrated.... I am sure I called a kid out and made them feel self-conscious. If I could go back and observe me as a principal, I would write myself up in evaluations, and I'd have very stern talks with myself, saying, "You're not going to be sarcastic with kids. You're not going to argue with kids. You're not going to make kids feel self-conscious by the way you're calling them out in class, and you're not going to raise your voice with kids." I have learned the hard way, but thankfully not through a bad evaluation or a stern "talking-to" by my boss or anything; but I did have to learn that if I wanted to be successful. A lot of teachers aren't willing to learn that, unfortunately.

—Jon, Veteran Middle School Teacher

 ## ANSWERING THE "WHO" QUESTION:
A 100-Word Reflection

How do you feel when students don't learn what you intended to teach them? What do you do when this happens? _____

_____

_____

_____

_____

_____

? ANSWERING THE "WHAT" QUESTION:
What the Research Tells Us

Professional Accountability for Learning:
What It Means

In this chapter we describe what we mean by professional accountability for learning and its relationship to self-efficacy. We begin, however, with the "flip side" of the accountability coin—the endemic blaming of students and families that goes on in too many schools. When we are conducting workshops, Bill often asks educators, "Is blaming happening in your school? When kids don't succeed, do you blame their parents? Do you blame each other?" Many people nod their heads and others seem surprised by the question. Naming the problem can make people uncomfortable.

We also ask the question, "Why do educators blame students, their families, or each other?" Most often we get honest answers: it's easier than taking responsibility, educators are afraid of looking incompetent, or they are frustrated after trying every strategy in their repertoire. Teachers may feel forced into choosing, albeit many times unconsciously, between "defining themselves as inadequate or the children as lacking..." (Haberman, 1995, p. 51).

In addition to these reasons for blame, we suggest another: too many educators simply do not believe they are accountable to *all* students. These educators reason that some students face too many barriers such as those posed by poverty. Some, they say, are lazy and others are not capable of learning (at least not to the level called for in most state's standards). Many say students do not have support at home. The "no support at home" rationale is augmented by the belief that parents, particularly those who live in poverty, do not care about their children's education.

What we believe about ourselves as educators, our students, and their families is "deeply coupled" with our sense of responsibility for learning (Diamond et al., 2004, p. 82). Teachers who do not assume responsibility for learning are fixated on student and family deficits and point to them as the reason for their instructional decisions and students' failure to achieve (Diamond et al., 2004). They provide less challenging work, assign highly structured activities, and are reluctant to embrace and try new instructional strategies (Diamond et al., 2004). On the other hand, those who hold themselves professionally accountable for learning (their students' learning and their own) go "back to the drawing board" when students fail to learn. They are persistent, creative, curious problem solvers (Haberman, 1995). As Lizzy, who teaches high school, said,

> I take time out to sit down and speak with students and figure out what is holding them back from being able to perform. A lot of times for me, I self-reflect. So, in regard to my teaching style, if my students don't do well, I am looking at what I did or what I can do to make things a little bit better, or what I didn't do to bring something across to them.

Teachers who hold themselves professionally accountable to *all* students are aware of the many ways poverty adversely influences their students' lives and learning. Still, rather than focus on what they cannot control, teachers who disrupt poverty focus on what they *can* control. This attribute is the most powerful predictor of a teacher's success with students who live in poverty (Haberman, 1995). These teachers see beyond the barriers poverty poses to the potential in the child. They emphasize students' assets rather than deficits and hold high expectations for them. They encourage students to learn challenging content; they make changes in instruction to meet students' needs; they draw on students' interests and passions to engage and motivate them; and they provide students who need it with additional time to demonstrate what they know and can do (Diamond et al., 2004).

Viewing ourselves as professionally accountable to students translates into a sense of responsibility for student learning that is not easily dismissed. In fact, educators who hold themselves accountable to *all* students are hard-pressed and highly averse to relinquishing responsibility for learning. When students fail to learn due to factors largely outside their control, these teachers find it painful, and they continue to question what more they (and the school as a system) might have done.

Antidotes to Blame: Self-Efficacy and Self-Awareness

The best antidote for blame is building self-efficacy, because there is a strong relationship between self-efficacy and professional responsibility for student learning (Guskey, 1982, 1988).

Self-Efficacy: What It Is and Why It Matters

More than four decades ago, researchers from the RAND Corporation added the following two items to a survey for teachers: (1) "When it comes right down to it, a teacher really can't do much because most of a student's motivation and performance depends on his or her home environment," and (2) "If I try really hard, I can get through to even the most difficult or unmotivated students" (Armor et al., 1976). Teachers indicated their degree of agreement or disagreement with the two statements, and their responses led to powerful findings and the conceptualization of teacher self-efficacy.

Guskey and Passaro (1994) define self-efficacy as "teachers' belief or conviction that they can influence how well students learn, even those who may be difficult or unmotivated" (p. 4). Teachers judge their personal competence to perform a teaching task in light of the demands of that particular task in a given context. They can feel "more or less efficacious under different circumstances" (Tschannen-Moran, Hoy, & Hoy, 1998, pp. 227–228).

Self-efficacy is correlated with teacher persistence and resilience (Ashton & Webb, 1986), willingness to use innovative approaches (Guskey, 1988; Smylie, 1988), willingness to work longer with struggling students (Gibson & Dembo, 1984), and greater enthusiasm for teaching (Guskey, 1988). Teachers with a strong sense of self-efficacy are less negative (Ashton, Webb, & Doda, 1982) and less critical of students (Ashton & Webb, 1986). Self-efficacy is also correlated with improved student achievement (Ashton & Webb, 1986).

Developing Self-Efficacy

Educators in each of the high-poverty, high-performing schools we studied for our previous book spoke of the intense level of professional learning occurring in their schools. "Growing teachers' knowledge and skills" was consistently identified as key to the schools' turnaround. Self-efficacy can be developed when teachers begin with an assessment of their competencies, are provided opportunities to practice new strategies with coaches who provide specific feedback, and are given time to collaborate with colleagues (Tschannen-Moran et al., 1998). Even then, when learning something new, teachers are likely to experience a dip in confidence at first and may need support to get through the learning curve (Guskey, 1986).

It has been our experience that educators continue to search for a set of strategies, approaches, or methods designed "just for kids in poverty." It may be comforting to some and distressing to others, but there is no such thing. Good teaching for all students is good teaching for students who live in poverty. Nonetheless, to do what successful teachers do requires us to understand not only the strategies and techniques they use, but also the theories that underpin their practice. For those wanting to build their sense of efficacy with students who live in poverty and wondering where to start, we make the following three suggestions: (1) attend to the theory behind human learning and motivation in both your instruction and your management of the classroom learning environment, (2) increase your expertise and repertoire in research-based practices, and (3) build reflection into your daily practice. We understand this recommendation is a career-long endeavor many of you have already undertaken; nonetheless, in what follows we provide a few resources to consider.

Thinking About Learning Theory with Ned's Gr8 8. It would be impossible to include in a few paragraphs everything educators might want or need to know about learning theory. However, in our workshops, we often use a brief animated YouTube video (http://www.youtube.com/watch?feature=player_embedded&v=p_BskcXTqpM) based on *Mind, Brain, and Education* by Hinton, Fischer, and Glennon (2012). In the video, Ned, a "talking teenage head," outlines what he calls his "Gr8 8"—eight learning principles based on neuroscience. An executive summary and the full report can be found at the Students at the Center website (http://studentsatthecenterhub.org/wp-content/uploads/2010/01/Mind-Brain-Education-Students-at-the-Center-1.pdf), and a review of the video with explanation of Ned's Gr8 8 can be found at http://www.whatkidscando.org/featurestories/2013/01_how_youth_learn/. Figure 6.1 summarizes Ned's eight principles.

Our point is not to suggest that knowing these eight learning principles will make you an expert in learning theory; rather, we want to encourage you to reflect on what you know about how people learn and how much you base what you do in your classroom on such theory. Think about students who struggle, some of whom may live in poverty. How many of your units, lessons, and activities are grounded in Ned's Gr8 8? If you are a principal, an instructional coach, or in another role intended to support teachers, do you have protocols in place to provide teachers with opportunities to reflect on the learning theory underpinning their practice?

FIGURE 6.1 | "Ned's Gr8 8": Eight Learning Principles

1. I feel OK.

"Emotion is fundamental to learning... If learning experiences are positive, students will be motivated to engage in them... If learning experiences are riddled with stress or other negative emotions, students will jump through hoops to avoid them."

2. It matters.

"Relevance is necessary for learning." Information that is not relevant to an individual's goals does not prompt "changes in brain circuitry thought to underlie learning."

3. It's active.

"Active engagement is necessary for learning." Passive exposure to information does not prompt "changes in brain circuitry thought to underlie learning... Students will learn more effectively when they are actively engaged in learning activities that they care about."

4. It stretches me.

"The brain continually adapts to experiences, a property neuroscientists call plasticity... As students learn, these experiences gradually sculpt connection among neurons in the brain."

5. I have a coach.

Learning happens over time and needs to be supported by a coach throughout the process.

6. I have to use it.

Connections among neurons that are most often used are strengthened; those used least are weakened. Ned says: "Use It or lose It. Students need opportunities to reinforce their learning." Formative assessment is a common form of reinforcement.

7. I think back on it.

Students need opportunities to reflect on their learning.

8. I plan my next steps.

Reflection on their learning should be used to inform students' "next steps" as learners.

Source: Adapted from the animated video *Ned's GR8 8* and a review by Christina Hinton, EdD entitled *Neuroscience Backs Up Ned's Gr8 8* accessed on April 20, 2017, from http://www.whatkidscando.org/featurestories/2013/01_how_youth_learn/.

Expanding Your Expertise: 10 Suggested Research-Based Practices. Many students who live in poverty do not have access to the quality of education afforded their more affluent peers, which severely constricts their life chances (see Anyon, 1985, 2005; Finn, 2009; Haberman, 1995). Haberman (1991) coined the phrase "pedagogy of poverty" to describe the teaching acts he observed in classrooms in the high-poverty schools he studied. His characterization of these acts can be summarized as teacher-centered, control-oriented, and managerially focused on student tasks of low-cognitive demand. Figure 6.2 is a compilation of 10 practices supported by empirical research. In contrast to a pedagogy of poverty, use of these practices establishes a pedagogy of possibility intended to nurture the potential in all learners.

As we previously mentioned, developing self-efficacy begins with assessing your competencies (Tschannen-Moran et al., 1998). Which of the practices in Figure 6.2 do you currently employ? Do you feel your use of those practices is effective? Why or why not? Which might you like to learn more about, and why? What do you hope to be able to do more of, or to do differently or better, by gaining new or additional expertise? Answering such questions is an example of reflective practice.

Self-Awareness: The Power of Reflective Practice

We have known for decades that "[t]heories of professional practice… determine all deliberate behavior" (Argyris & Schön, 1974, p. 7). Throughout this book we have encouraged you to write 100-word reflections, use reflection tools, and engage in dialogue with colleagues. All of these activities are intended to help you answer the who, why, how, and what questions, because these questions are at the heart of both theories-of-action and theories-in-use.

David Schön (1983), author of *The Reflective Practitioner: How Professionals Think in Action*, describes two types of reflection teachers need to do to improve their practice: reflection *in* action and reflection *on* action. In essence, the first is reflecting *while* teaching and the second is reflecting *before* or *after* teaching. Espousing a theoretical stance for our practice does not mean our practice is actually consistent with the espoused theory. For most of us, there is a gap between our espoused theory and our practice. We know, however, that "theory is only useful when it is applied and developed in practice" (Scales, 2013, p. 12). This application requires reflection both in and on our practice. As teachers experiment with their theories and reflect on their experiences, their practice improves.

FIGURE 6.2 | Ten Effective Practices for Developing a Pedagogy of Possibility

Effective Practices Backed by 40 Years of Research	
1. Teach, model, and provide experiences that develop creative and critical thinking skills. • Creating "maker spaces" • Teaching innovation design protocols • Asking open-ended questions • Using problem-based learning scenarios • Employing Socratic seminars • Developing multidisciplinary units • Integrating technology • Integrating the arts throughout the curriculum • STEM and STEAM	• Barton, Tan, & Greenberg (2017) • Eisenman & Payne (1997) • Johannessen (2004) • Langer (2001) • Ornelles (2007) • Pogrow (2005) • Schlichter, Hobbs, & Crump (1988) • Sheridan et al. (2014) • Wagner & Dintersmith (2015)
2. Prioritize literacy development. • Preteaching vocabulary • Engaging in word study • Accessing and building on prior knowledge • Embracing the reading and writing connection • Teaching, modeling, and practicing academic discourse • Focusing on meaning-making • Integrating literacy across the curriculum	• Edmondson & Shannon (1998) [in Milner] • Johannessen (2004) • Kameenui & Carnine (1998) • Knapp & Adelman (1995) • Lareau (1987) • Milner (2015) • Rockwell (2007) • Routman (2014)
3. Foster belonging and create a bond between students and school. • Conducting morning/class meetings • Facilitating team-building activities, particularly at the beginning of the year • Intentionally building relationships with students • Providing positive behavior supports • Facilitating cooperative learning, peer tutoring, and mentoring	• Benner, Nelson, Sanders, & Ralston (2012) • Rudge & Parrott (2000) • Comer (1993) • Craig (2016) • Lalas (2007) • Langer (2001) • Luthar & Becker (2002) • Milner (2015)
4. Personalize instruction based on learning needs, interests, and aspirations. • Mediating and scaffolding learning experiences through— — "think-alouds" — reciprocal teaching — visual organizers and models — guided practice — sheltered instruction	

FIGURE 6.2 | Ten Effective Practices for Developing a Pedagogy of Possibility
—(*continued*)

Effective Practices Backed by 40 Years of Research	
• Differentiating instruction • Fostering multiple intelligences • Providing for student choice in all phases of the learning process • Connecting students' aspirations to learning • Integrating arts throughout the curriculum	• Campbell & Campbell (1999) • Echevarría, Vogt, & Short (2004) • Honigsfeld & Dunn (2009) • Johannessen (2004) • Palinscar & Brown (1985) • Pogrow (2006) • Quaglia & Fox (2003) • Tomlinson et al. (2003)
5. Actively engage students in learning experiences for authentic, relevant purposes, which can help them envision their futures and foster hope. • Engaging in project-based learning • Engaging in place-based learning (service learning, environmental education, community-based learning, outdoor education, indigenous education, internships, apprenticeships, entrepreneurial activities) • Teaching concepts and using formative assessment focused on deep levels of understanding • Employing student-led conferencing • Engaging in expeditionary learning	• Bailey & Guskey (2000) • Boaler (2002) • Bodilly et. al. (1998) • Furco & Root (2010) • Kinsley (1997) • Newmann, Bryk, & Nagaoka (2001) • Smith & Sobel (2010) • Williams (2003)
6. Use "teacher language" that supports academic learning, develops self-control, and builds community. Using language to— • develop a growth mindset in students • provide feedback that encourages students to "own" their learning • help students self-monitor their behavior • build social skills • positively redirect students • help students identify their strengths • promote positive identity development • develop a sense of efficacy and agency in students	• Denton (2013) • Johnston (2004, 2012)

FIGURE 6.2 | Ten Effective Practices for Developing a Pedagogy of Possibility —(continued)

Effective Practices Backed by 40 Years of Research	
7. Teach, model, and practice social and emotional skills. • Developing skills in conflict resolution, collaboration, communication, and adaptability • Developing the ability to recognize, express, and manage emotions • Developing the ability to see others' perspectives • Using trauma-sensitive strategies • Employing mindfulness practices and other stress-reducing techniques • Emphasizing a growth mindset • Developing character and citizenship	• Black & Fernando (2014) • Buckner, Mezzacappa, & Beardslee (2009) • Claro, Paunesku, & Dweck (2016) • Craig (2016)
8. Develop executive-functioning skills. • Using multisensory instruction • Providing memory aids such as mnemonic devices • Teaching brainstorming, forecasting, and planning • Using graphic organizers • Using semantic mapping • Teaching study skills • Chunking information • Building "habits of mind"	• Costa & Kallick (2009) • Fogarty (2009) • Hyerle (2009) • Jensen (2009) • Schlichter, Hobbs, & Crump (1988)
9. Integrate physical activity, exercise, and movement into teaching and learning. • Setting fitness goals and monitoring progress • Focusing physical education on lifelong sports and fitness • Preserving recess time • Integrating movement into the teaching of academic subjects • Using stress reduction techniques such as time out, breathing, yoga	• Dariotis et al. (2016) • Lindt & Miller (2017) • Pellegrini & Bohn (2005) • Sibley & Etnier (2003)
10. Develop students' awareness of bias, discrimination, and injustice. • Preserving social studies and civic education in the schedule • Teaching about the history of poverty and classism • Reading picture books and novels about empowered working-class families and those living in poverty • Using an anti-bias curriculum • Participating in poverty simulations • Engaging in problem-based learning to address local issues	• Gorski (2013) • Lalas (2007) • Milner (2015)

"Reflection can be difficult, even threatening, because it forces us to be honest with ourselves and recognize not only our successes but areas where we need to improve. It makes us take responsibility for our teaching and learning" (Scales, 2013, p. 16). Celia told us,

> I think mindset is the very first thing. If your mindset isn't right, if you don't think students can achieve it, then they won't because that's the way you'll operate when you're working with kids. Second thing is understanding your own biases. Understanding what you bring personally as a teacher into the classroom, and being as honest with yourself as possible. You can't be afraid to call yourself out when you're being biased. You can't teach if you are sleepwalking.

Most models proposed for teacher reflection are iterative and cyclical—they entail learning by doing. In *Teach, Reflect, Learn: Building Your Capacity for Success in the Classroom,* Pete Hall and Alisa Simeral (2015) propose a "working definition" for self-reflection, which "includes an overarching concept (i.e., the act of exerting mental energy about our professional responsibilities) and a series of very specific reflective behaviors:

- Gaining awareness of our educational surroundings (students, content, and pedagogy).
- Planning deliberately and taking action with intentionality.
- Assessing the impact of our decisions and actions.
- Adjusting our course of action based on the feedback we receive from those assessments.
- Engaging in this reflective cycle continuously. (pp. 14–15)

Multiple iterations of this cycle, they assert, move us to increased self-awareness on a continuum from *unaware* to *conscious* to *action*—and finally, to *refinement.*

In his book, *Star Teachers of Children in Poverty,* Haberman (1995) concluded it was impossible to learn from the successful teachers he studied by simply attempting to replicate their actions. The manner in which they *thought* about their practice was inseparable from their actions. In fact, it was the theories that guided their practice that differentiated them from those who were unsuccessful (or less successful) with students who live in poverty. We found the same to be true of the teachers we interviewed. It did not take long to understand that their theories made them successful.

Among the many theories that guide successful teachers, as we stated earlier, is the belief that they can successfully teach *all* children and it is their responsibility to do so.

 ANSWERING THE "HOW" QUESTION:
Tips from Teachers

Six Practical Suggestions to Hold Yourself Professionally Accountable for Student Learning

Educators who view themselves as accountable to every student do everything they can to authentically involve parents and families, work to build self-efficacy in students, and commit to their own continued growth. In what follows, the educators we interviewed offer six suggestions to consider in doing so.

1. Focus on What You Can Control

Most of the teachers we interviewed talked about the need to focus on what they could control. For example, Celia said to us,

> I take each student's learning as my personal responsibility. I am responsible, not their parents. It's not about what the parents can or can't do or what neighborhoods they do or don't live in. At the end of day, I do what I can within my sphere of influence.

Doing what they can within their sphere of influence, as Mary described it, was often about "finding a way to still teach the kids, whatever they are going through, and helping them progress by meeting them where they are."

Being persistent and having a "back to the drawing board" attitude when students failed to learn what they had been taught was another way these teachers exerted influence. Lizzy's theory of action was indicative of others':

> I self-reflect and see what it is that I can do better, because it's always something. It's not that kids just don't want to do it. I feel like it's something that I can literally figure out. And I sit down and have a conversation about it with them. I just keep trying.

2. Be Open to Critique and Willing to Learn

Holding ourselves accountable entails being open to critique and willingness to learn. Many of those interviewed shared the many ways they had grown and changed throughout their careers. Alex spoke of becoming more patient and learning not to take things personally. He described how, as a beginning teacher, it was "all about him." He said, "I would take credit when they succeeded, but blame them when they failed. Now it's about giving. That's it." Celia also relayed her story of professional growth and offered some advice. She suggested,

> Don't be afraid to ask for help. Build a relationship with someone who you see as a more outstanding teacher and glean from those people. The first year that I worked with my accountability partner, all my years of experience got in the way. Since she's younger, she'd gone through the credentialing program more recently... maybe 15 years later than I did, so she had picked up on some other tools. She looked at me and said, "Celia, you're not doing what's in the best interest of these kids because you don't believe in it. You don't think it works, but you need to try it." Coming from her and knowing what kind of relationship we had, I said, "OK, fine. You tell me what to do, you come and observe, see if it works, and if it doesn't, give me something else to try." And so, it's been really good.

3. Find an Accountability Partner

Celia continued,

> Getting an accountability partner to talk things through when things come up is important. You have to have a space where people can call you out, not in a bad way, but can say, "Hey, that doesn't look like the best use of the kids' time," or "that doesn't seem like the best reading for that." You have to have trust and allow for your colleagues to look at your practice and give you feedback. I don't understand the kind of school that lets me be in my own classroom and no one comes in to see what I'm doing. That's a recipe for disaster.

In Celia's case, working with an "accountability partner" was the way "they did business" in her school. In other instances, it was completely voluntary. Teachers told us that working with a partner helped them get to, and stay at the top of, their game. As Alex explained,

We knew we weren't the best, but we knew we had a lot of potential. We had a lot of success, but we really wanted to just push the envelope and raise the bar ourselves. I wanted somebody who would be able to listen to me, because I knew that I could probably solve my own problems. I just needed somebody to listen so I could do that.

Jon also had an accountability partner. He and his partner taught at different schools, so they met once a week early in the morning at a coffee shop.

We talk about our goals for the year and how to be accountable and consistent about reaching those goals. "Don't fade out. Stay strong. Stick with it." We told each other those things. We even read books together, like *Positive Deviance* and *Switch*. We met up once a week at a coffee shop or at his house or whatever. We would just share our tough times and our victories. We'd be like, "Hey, why don't you try this? Or why don't you try that?" I think there's too many teachers who are lone rangers in the classroom and don't want to be accountable to anyone.

4. Let Students Know You Won't Give Up on Them

As we described previously in this chapter, helping students gain a strong sense of efficacy leads them to "ownership" and self-regulation of their learning. Part of holding yourself accountable for learning is helping students hold themselves accountable too. For those who live in poverty, particularly generational poverty, they may come to you having "learned the lessons" we described earlier—life just happens and they have no control; failure is predictable; the future is uncertain; and the criteria for success in life are unclear. In one way or another, most of the teachers we interviewed described the importance of believing in students, even when they did not believe in themselves, and letting them know that they would not give up on them. For instance, Miranda said,

By the end of the year, Guillermo was talking with the other classmates despite his little stutter; his stutter even got a little better. He was more confident in himself, and I 100 percent believe that it was because he knew that I believed in him. And I would tell him every time he took a test, "You might not believe in yourself; but I believe in you." I tell my students, "I believe in you guys. Even if you don't believe you can do it, I believe you can do it, so just think about that."

Many told us they remind their students regularly that "everyone makes mistakes" and "learning takes practice." Celia's comment illuminated this point.

> A difficult student who doesn't want to follow classroom rules and wants to be defiant and just doesn't want to work—I don't give up on that kid. I continue to try to build a relationship. I continue to try to connect with the kids. I share my own personal stories of when I was in elementary school. I am very honest with them and say, "Hey, I wasn't the best student. I got in trouble, but you can change. You can do the work. You can work hard. I will never quit on you. Hang in there with me. I am not going to quit on you."

Others found their own colleagues to be one of their greatest challenges. Many of them spoke of teachers giving up on students—"writing them off." Jon shared this observation:

> The thing that is the biggest obstacle for me is previous relationships with other teachers who haven't been positive with the students. I think the teachers before me did a great job teaching their content, but they didn't build relationships. They came to this school to teach, they said, not build relationships. It takes a while for the kids to get to know me . . . to know that I am not going to give up on them. The kids need to see that we love them and we suffer with them; that we're there for them.

5. Consider Yourself on the Same Team as Your Students

The teachers we interviewed for this book viewed themselves as being on the same team as their students. This characteristic, in particular, sets them apart from teachers who are less successful with students who struggle. There is no "them and me" mentality in their classroom. Martin Haberman (1995) described this attribute as the "You and me against the material" function of successful teachers. For example, in David's classroom, he told us,

> They're all going to at least be reading at grade level by the time they leave me. If they are already there, they're going to be reading as high as we (the students and I) can get them. If we're talking math, I assess where they are in math and we start filling the gaps. I'm not doing my job if they aren't leaving 5th grade at a 5th grade level. If they aren't, then that's on me. If they get an *F*, I get an *F*.

6. Take Risks

One of the many ways these teachers grow their sense of efficacy is by taking risks. As a first-year teacher, Leslie took it upon herself to develop and operate a summer camp to welcome 60 new students, all of whom were refugees. She described this experience as building her confidence:

> It took a lot of courage for me to do. I was a new teacher, but I was very passionate about what we were doing. I kind of jumped in head first and said, "I want to do this, and I think this is important. And I think we need to do this." And I was very scared that I would be shot down, or other teachers who had been teaching much longer than I had, or had more experience with ELL students, would shoot me down. But they didn't. We worked together and embraced it. I think that helped me feel more confident as an educator.

During summer school, Jon assumed the role of summer school principal and was quickly presented with a dilemma that tested him. He explained,

> A kid passed out some of his medication that was in his backpack from a camping trip. The first thing he asks is, "You're going to kick me out, aren't you?" Kids automatically think that we're out to get them. So I have to break down those barriers and get them to realize, "No, I'm your advocate. I'm here to support you." Instead of kicking him out of summer school, I put together an in-house summer school program called Turning Point, where kids are 100 percent supervised, and they get the work sent in from the teachers. They're not kicked out of summer school, but they are being disciplined. They still have to do community service throughout the day. They still have the potential to earn their credits and move on and promote to the next grade, or get the credit and graduate on time. It's all about not giving up on them and sticking with them, being there for them.

Jon explained that he took a lot of flack from his colleagues for implementing the Turning Point program. He said,

> It took courage. I got some pretty scathing e-mails from my colleagues, even though I had presented the idea to them. The kids had to wear separate T-shirts to identify them for safety reasons. And they couldn't be without an adult. Teachers told me, "I feel completely unsupported; I feel like I want to walk out." In the end, I've got to be able to go to sleep at night and feel good about what I am doing for these kids. Like I told you, I'm helping kids who are like me and my sisters... it's personal.

For more specific ideas for fostering professional accountability, see Figure 6.3.

FIGURE 6.3 | Ideas for Fostering Professional Accountability

Harness the Power of the Group—Building collective efficacy can promote a norm of professional responsibility for student learning. Use formal structures such as grade-level teams, departments, or professional learning communities (PLCs) to develop collective efficacy. Build ownership for students as a collective group.

Find an Accountability Partner—Find someone willing to be an accountability partner. Each partner should set goals. Meet regularly for discussion, problem solving, and encouragement.

Be Transparent in Practice—Commit to transparency in professional practice and in results. Model in your practice the idea that failure is normal. Learn from the lessons that flop and share your learning with others.

Employ "Push, Pull, Nudge"—Those who effectively support teachers' growth employ all three—pushing, pulling, and nudging. It requires that participants suspend judgment about where others are in current capacity and help move them forward. For additional information, see http://www.michaelfullan.ca/wp-content/uploads/2013/08/JSD-Power-of-Professional-Capital.pdf.

Remember Kindergarten—Sharing is important. Give your best ideas away.

You Can't Teach Sleepwalking—As one teacher said, "You can't teach sleepwalking," suggesting teachers needed to make reflection a professional habit. Develop a lens through which to think about instruction by developing a rich set of three or four questions to routinely ask yourself. Employ the questions before, during, and after instruction.

Know Yourself—Ask yourself the "who" question on a regular basis—Who am I as a teacher? Who am I through the eyes of my students and my colleagues? Commit to identifying your biases and blind spots by challenging your mental maps.

Turn to Wonder—The next time a student or a parent does something you do not understand, turn from judgment to "wonderment." Instead of judging their behavior as good or bad, moral or immoral, responsible or irresponsible, ask yourself, "I wonder why they did that?"

Be Nice, Work Hard—The principal of a school we recently visited told us the school's "rules" were *Be Nice, Work Hard*. Encourage personal responsibility among students and professional responsibility in adults by promoting the simple values of being kind and working hard.

There is no getting around it: teaching is "heart work"; teaching is courageous. The root word for courage is *cor*, which is the Latin word for "heart." *Courage*, according to the *American Heritage Dictionary*, 4th edition, is "the state or quality of mind or spirit that enables one to face danger, fear, or vicissitudes with self-possession, confidence, and resolution...." Such a definition describes teachers who disrupt poverty. In Chapter 7, we turn to the subject of courage.

APPLYING YOUR LEARNING TO YOUR PRACTICE

- Think of the times when you have felt most effective as a teacher. What factors were at play?
- From your perspective, what does it mean to have "a sense of efficacy" as an educator?

Application of Learning Matrix

To help you apply what you are learning to your professional practice, see Appendix A. Each chapter's high-leverage question is listed there, with space to list each student and reflect on what you know. Teachers with more than 25 students may want to use multiple matrices or select a particular class period. For this chapter, here is the high-leverage question: What do I do when _____ [student's name] doesn't learn something I have taught?

Challenging Our Mental Maps:
Learning, Unlearning, and Relearning Summary

Pause for a few minutes and use the following questions to consider your current thinking as it relates to the information and ideas presented in this chapter.

Learning: What conceptions did you hold about professional accountability for learning before reading this chapter?

Unlearning: How, if at all, did the chapter challenge your beliefs or thinking?

Relearning: How might this "challenge to your thinking" or new idea be beneficial or helpful to you?

Action: What action will you take, and why?

As you consider your answers and progress through this book, record your answers for each chapter in the summary table supplied in Appendix B. The summary table provides you with a model for exploring your mental map, reflecting on current practice, developing your theory of action, and planning next steps.

COMMUNITIES OF PRACTICE:
Extending Your Learning with Others

- Reflect upon the way educators talk about students who under-achieve and live in poverty in your school. List 5 to 10 statements you have heard. Based on these statements, what would you conclude about educators' sense of efficacy in your school?
- How would we as colleagues define professional accountability for learning?
- What are examples of blame occurring in our school?
- How are we employing "Ned's Gr8 8"?
- To what degree are we currently using the 10 practices suggested in Figure 6.2?
- What do we think about the value of accountability partners?
- Do all of our students know we won't give up on them? How do we know?

Challenging Stereotypes to Accept Professional Accountability

Stereotype 5: People in poverty do not value education.

The belief that people in poverty do not value education is one of the most prominent stereotypes in our society, despite the ample evidence (four decades of studies) to the contrary (Gorski, 2012). As educators, we do not live outside our societal culture; and so, given the prominence of this stereotype, that culture is likely to influence our mental maps related to the topic at hand—professional accountability for learning.

In her article "Recognizing and Welcoming the Standpoint of Low-Income Parents in the Public Schools," Bernice Lott (2003) points to numerous studies that demonstrate that people who live in poverty link their children's hopes and dreams to success in school, even when they mistrust schools as a result of their own negative experiences. "The dominant view held by teachers and administrators that the parents of low-income children care less about their children's education than middle-class parents and resist active involvement is not supported by quantitative or qualitative data" (Lott, 2003, p. 253). Instead, studies demonstrate that low-income families are concerned about their children's academic achievement and would like to be involved in their children's schooling; nonetheless, the resources available to these families to "follow through on their desire to help their children negotiate success in school" are severely constrained (Lott, 2003, p. 254).

One factor that contributes to the perpetuation of this stereotype is educators' limited notion of what "valuing" education looks like (Gorski, 2012). Many view parental involvement as what happens "at school." Research confirms that parents who live in poverty are less likely to be involved in at-school activities (Mattingly et al., 2002, as cited in Gorski, 2012); nonetheless, this does not mean they value education any more or less than parents who do not live in poverty. Parents who live in poverty face many real barriers to such involvement—long working hours, no paid leave, child care constraints, limited options for transportation, and, for undocumented parents, fear of discovery (Gorski, 2012; Lott, 2003).

Studies also document that parents living in poverty are dissuaded from involvement within schools by the unwelcoming and judgmental environment many schools project to low-income families. Lott's (2003) article chronicles a wealth of studies that demonstrate that too many schools discount low-income parents' perspectives, treat their children in ways that mirror the way the parents were treated in school, and respond to students in a judgmental and demeaning manner. Additionally, low-income parents may be unsure how to help their children and unsure what questions to ask (Fine, 1993, as cited in Lott, 2003), and they may be afraid to ask for help because they are concerned about being judged (Keller & McDade, 2000).

Lareau (1987) found middle-class and low-income parents behave differently when visiting their children's classrooms. Low-income parents are much more hesitant. Their awareness of differences in education, income, and occupational status pose challenges in viewing teachers as equals. Additionally, middle-class parents' social and cultural capital enables them to advocate for customization in their children's education, whereas low-income parents are not afforded the same privilege (Lareau, 1987, as cited in Lott, 2003).

These studies not only point to the fallaciousness of this stereotype, but also present educators with a challenge. Would this stereotype be so unquestionably accepted if we were to make a concerted effort to heed the call scholars have laid out for us, such as expanding our ideas about what constitutes "valuing education," and making our "at school" involvement more welcoming for low-income parents and families by hearing and respecting their perspectives? As Lott (2003) points out, "Parents can be particularly helpful as sources of knowledge about their children—a source often ignored by schools" (p. 96). Yet this will only happen when communication is two-way and respect is mutual, or in Lott's words, when teachers are no longer just the "knowers" and parents are no longer just the "receivers" (p. 97). After all, there is no social justice without voice (Guyton, 2000, as cited in Lott, 2003).

VOICES FROM POVERTY

ANNA

Both my parents were in and out of prison all my life. Drugs. I grew up in that situation, and I've kind of seen it all.

My parents moved out west to hopefully work on their marriage, but my dad was more into the drug scene, and it became more important to him once we moved out there. That's when he and my mom got a divorce and he got arrested. He went to prison and didn't get out until I was about 11.

It was a very abusive situation. I was 5 years old, and when they started fighting, the first thing I would say was, "Hey, let's pack our bags." I knew we had to leave. I was always having to bounce around, not having a real place to stay. I just didn't know for sure where we were going to be sleeping at night. And experiencing that abuse was hard because he would hit her and verbally abuse her. The only reason they were together was because of the drug situation.

My mom was also using and actually got arrested on drug charges. She spent 30 days in jail

and I think a few years on probation and house arrest. I grew up watching people use drugs, people stealing, and all kinds of stuff. I experienced it all.

As a little kid, I was put in SPED. I think it was about 5th grade when I started to realize that having to leave the room to get that extra instruction was embarrassing. I went to the SPED teacher at my next IEP and explained to her that it was kind of embarrassing. It seemed like she just put so much effort into me. She would keep me after school to help me. She would just make sure I got that extra push that I needed. She acted as if she cared. It helped, but I was still in SPED.

In middle school, I decided I didn't want to be down there anymore. I didn't want to be in SPED when I was in high school. We set my goal high, and she said, "If you work hard, you can test out and just be in a regular room." And you know what? I worked my little butt off, and I did.

I had a job the minute I turned 16 my freshman year of high school. I think even at one point I had two jobs. But then my mom got arrested and was sentenced about the middle of my sophomore year. She got eight years in federal prison.

There were two years where we didn't even get to see her and only had contact by phone and e-mail. I'm really close with my mom. She's probably one of my best friends. Her being gone was really hard. Pretty much through high school I was on my own. I lived with my mom's boyfriend, but it was just a place to stay. He didn't pay for my cell phone. He didn't help with groceries. Going to high school and then having a full-time job on top of that at night serving tables, it was really, really hard.

To be totally honest, I didn't see myself being a teacher growing up. I went to my counselor for my classes, and she suggested trying a practicum. I jumped in and did my first practicum and fell in love with it. I fell in love with being around kids and teaching kids who were a lot like me in the high-poverty school where I did my practicum.

I got my degree in special education as well as regular education. After I graduated, I moved back home. I got a job in my neighboring town as a 1st grade teacher, and that was my dream job.

I think at our school a lot of us understand where a lot of these kids come from and what their parents are like. We have a family that is very poor, and it doesn't even look like they shower or take a bath at all. The school opens up the showers in the locker rooms for them, and just hearing some of the things—you just have to tell those other teachers not to be so judgmental.

Just hearing those comments, it's like, "Oh my God, those parents. I can't believe they'd do that." You have to be able to relate with that. A lot of these teachers never grew up wondering when the next meal was going to come and don't understand that sometimes you don't have the money for stuff. ■

7 DISRUPTION 5: HAVING THE COURAGE AND WILL TO TAKE ACTION

It takes courage to grow up and become who you really are.

—e.e. cummings

Several years ago, Kathleen attended a training session for educators selected to serve as consultants to Title I schools in a five-state region of the northwestern United States. The speaker, an attractive, well-dressed Distinguished Educator (literally, that was her title) from Kentucky had described the work she and her colleagues were doing to support struggling schools. As she ended her presentation, she began to talk about her personal calling as a teacher.

She lowered her voice, took a deep breath, and began to tell her story. She had lived a privileged life, raising her only child, a daughter, in gated communities, eventually sending her to a prestigious university. At that point in the story she paused, took another deep breath and continued. Her daughter, she slowly and quietly explained, was raped and murdered during her freshman year. The room was silent. People began to cry. And then she said something that sticks with Kathleen to this day:

> I could be angry. I could be really angry; but I have decided not to be. Rather, I am committed to doing what I can to serve children who have not lived a privileged life, because until the world is better for all children, it will not be better for our children.

As we (Kathleen and Bill) reflect on her message today, we remain in awe of the courage and will to take action demonstrated by this educator. Throughout our study we have been drawn to so many examples of the courageous and willful actions taken by the teachers we interviewed in support of their students. Yet when asked about courage, every one of these teachers rejected the notion that *they* were courageous, choosing instead to apply that descriptor mostly to their students. When asked if she ever thought of herself as courageous, Connie replied, "No. I don't know if I could say that. I would maybe say courageous is something somebody else might say. I think of myself as determined and resilient."

We are also reminded of the heavy burden educators shoulder in advocating for their students. Nina described how she felt compelled to advocate for people who live in poverty. She relayed a conversation she had with her classmates in the master's program in which she was enrolled.

> They started talking about how people in poverty have a poor work ethic. I wanted to burst out in tears because I was pissed. Burst out in tears because I was offended. The hair on the back of my neck was standing, and it was like, "Wait a minute—this is me." I felt like they were saying I don't have a strong work ethic. "Growing up I worked my ass off to provide for myself and my family, and you're telling me you buy into that stigma?" I raised my hand. I love that I can advocate for myself now. I never felt like I could in the past. I raised my hand and I said, "Whoa, whoa, whoa. We, as a group of future leaders, really need to be careful about how we are thinking about this."

Courage and a willingness to take action, as Nina exemplified, relate directly to the significant, interdependent nature of our relationships with our colleagues and to the critical importance of public schooling. To this end, we turn to the wisdom John Dewey imparted a century ago:

> What the best and wisest parent wants for his own child, that must the community want for all of its children. Any other ideal for our schools is narrow and unlovely; acted upon, it destroys our democracy... only by being true to the full growth of all the individuals who make it up can society by any chance be true to itself. And in the self-direction thus given, nothing counts as much as the school.... (1915, pp. 11–12)

We are also reminded of the important role our personal moral purpose plays in our professional life. Educators, especially teachers, are seldom afforded the opportunity to discuss the principles upon which they base their professional practice or the reasons they do the work they do. Doris Santoro (2011) argues that bad policy has created a school environment in which teachers can no longer access the moral purposes that led them to become educators in the first place. Contrasting this phenomenon with teacher "burnout," she speaks of it as "de*moral*ization."

Our research in high-poverty, high-performing schools illuminates the absolute necessity for educators to tap into the moral purposes for their vocation frequently—even daily (Budge & Parrett, 2016; Parrett & Budge, 2009). The work is simply too overwhelming to not do so. Teachers and other educators in these schools speak of feeling needed. They describe a sense of loyalty to their students and their own values, and they say that knowing they make a difference helps to protect them from becoming demoralized.

Educators who disrupt poverty possess a matured, moral purpose for their professional practice. Their personal theories of action emanate from principled perspectives related to fairness and justice. This is so, in part, because they have acquired clarity about *who* they are as people and *why* they chose to become educators. At the same time, they also understand that "all the moral indignation in the world" is not enough. They must also be skilled in the *what* and the *how* questions.

Foundational to everything else, effective teachers build caring relationships of mutual respect and trust with students. They work to reject deficit perspectives of people who live in poverty because they are courageous enough to engage in reflection, particularly of their own biases and blind spots. This reflection makes it possible for them to establish high expectations and provide multiple supports to meet those expectations. A central means of supporting students who live in poverty is through ensuring equity in terms of the structures, processes, and practices employed in the classroom, including grading, testing, and the use of homework. When students fail to learn, these teachers, despite the significant effort they have already invested, go back to the drawing board. They do not blame students, their families, or other circumstances because they possess self-efficacy and confidence in their professional capacity, which makes it possible to hold themselves professionally accountable for learning.

Finally, the educators who disrupt poverty understand, as did the distinguished educator from Kentucky, *"There is no neutral space in this work"* (Milner, 2015, p. 11, emphasis in original). Studies demonstrate that most teachers "stick to their own classrooms" in terms of their social justice-oriented practice, focusing primarily on creating a supportive learning environment (McAllister & Irvine, 2002). Nonetheless, it can often be difficult for individual educators to tap into their moral purposes for any length of time without the support of their colleagues and the system itself. In *Turning High-Poverty Schools into High-Performing Schools,* we focused primarily on collaboration among colleagues and the school "as a system" supporting such collective action. Collective efficacy often gives rise to abandoning practices, mindsets, processes, and structures that perpetuate underachievement.

In this book, we have not abandoned the importance of collective action; rather, we begin with the individual teacher and move outward toward collective action (hence, the questions at the end of Chapters 2 through 6). The move from the individual to the collective was intentional, for there is much we can do as individual educators, but as we have attempted to communicate throughout this book, it takes courage to face ourselves. It takes humility and a willingness to be vulnerable. *It calls on us to have the courage to do what we can.* That may sound quite trite or inadequate, but when we pause to think about it, willfully doing what we can is incredibly powerful.

Think about the kind of schools we could build if we were all willing to do what we can for the children we serve. In the words of author Marianne Williamson,

> Our deepest fear is not that we are inadequate. Our deepest fear is that we are powerful beyond measure. It is our light, not our darkness that most frightens us... It is not just in some of us; it is in everyone, and as we let our own light shine, we unconsciously give others permission to do the same. (1992, p. 190)

It is within each of us that disrupting poverty begins.

APPENDIX A

Application of Learning Matrices

Directions: In each matrix, write the name of each student (one per box) and answer the high-leverage question in the space provided. Use the completed matrices to reflect on your practice and plan next steps.

High-Leverage Question:
What do I know about [student's name] living conditions?

Name:	Name:	Name:	Name:	Name:
Name:	Name:	Name:	Name:	Name:
Name:	Name:	Name:	Name:	Name:
Name:	Name:	Name:	Name:	Name:
Name:	Name:	Name:	Name:	Name:

Next Steps:

High-Leverage Question:
What assets, strengths, or cultural funds of knowledge does [student's name] bring to the classroom?

Name:	Name:	Name:	Name:	Name:
Name:	Name:	Name:	Name:	Name:
Name:	Name:	Name:	Name:	Name:
Name:	Name:	Name:	Name:	Name:
Name:	Name:	Name:	Name:	Name:

Next Steps:

High-Leverage Question:
What do I expect [student's name] to accomplish this year?

Name:	Name:	Name:	Name:	Name:
Name:	Name:	Name:	Name:	Name:
Name:	Name:	Name:	Name:	Name:
Name:	Name:	Name:	Name:	Name:
Name:	Name:	Name:	Name:	Name:

Next Steps:

High-Leverage Question:
Is [student's name] "school dependent"? If so, what does this student most need from school to level the playing field?

Name:	Name:	Name:	Name:	Name:
Name:	Name:	Name:	Name:	Name:
Name:	Name:	Name:	Name:	Name:
Name:	Name:	Name:	Name:	Name:
Name:	Name:	Name:	Name:	Name:

Next Steps:

High-Leverage Question:
What do I do when [student's name] doesn't learn something I have taught?

Name:	Name:	Name:	Name:	Name:
Name:	Name:	Name:	Name:	Name:
Name:	Name:	Name:	Name:	Name:
Name:	Name:	Name:	Name:	Name:
Name:	Name:	Name:	Name:	Name:

Next Steps:

APPENDIX B

Learning, Unlearning, and Relearning Summary Table

Directions: Use this table to summarize and capture your thinking as you read through the book, as well as to support your planning for taking action in your classroom.

Chapter 2 A Poverty Primer		
Learning	**Unlearning**	**Relearning**
What conceptions did you hold about poverty before reading this chapter?	How, if at all, did the chapter challenge your beliefs or thinking?	How might this "challenge to your thinking" or new idea be beneficial or helpful to you?

Chapter 3 Disruption 1: Building Caring Relationships and Advocating for Students		
Learning	**Unlearning**	**Relearning**
What conceptions did you hold about teacher expectations before reading this chapter?	How, if at all, did the chapter challenge your beliefs or thinking?	How might this "challenge to your thinking" or new idea be beneficial or helpful to you?

Source: © 2018 by ASCD. From *Disrupting Poverty: Five Powerful Classroom Practices* by K. M. Budge and W. H. Parrett. Readers may download and duplicate appendixes for noncommercial use within their school. See www.ascd.org/publications/books/116012.aspx

Chapter 4	Disruption 2: Holding High Expectations and Providing Needed Support	
Learning	**Unlearning**	**Relearning**
What conceptions did you hold about teacher expectations before reading this chapter?	How, if at all, did the chapter challenge your beliefs or thinking?	How might this "challenge to your thinking" or new idea be beneficial or helpful to you?

Chapter 5	Disruption 3: Committing to Equity	
Learning	**Unlearning**	**Relearning**
What conceptions did you hold about equity before reading this chapter?	How, if at all, did the chapter challenge your beliefs or thinking?	How might this "challenge to your thinking" or new idea be beneficial or helpful to you?

Chapter 6   Disruption 4: Accepting Professional Accountability for Learning

Learning	Unlearning	Relearning
What conceptions did you hold about professional accountability for learning before reading this chapter?	How, if at all, did the chapter challenge your beliefs or thinking?	How might this "challenge to your thinking" or new idea be beneficial or helpful to you?

Chapter 7   Disruption 5: Having the Will to Take Action

Learning + Unlearning + Relearning = Action

Look back upon the reflections you recorded on this summary table. How has your thinking changed? What actions will you take and why?

Source: © 2018 by ASCD. From *Disrupting Poverty: Five Powerful Classroom Practices* by K. M. Budge and W. H. Parrett. Readers may download and duplicate appendixes for noncommercial use within their school. See www.ascd.org/publications/books/116012.aspx

REFERENCES

Allington, R. L. (1980). Poor readers don't get to read much in reading groups. *Language Arts, 57*(8), 872–876.

Allington, R., & McGill-Franzen, A. (2008, April). Got books? *Educational Leadership, 65*(7), 20–23.

Annie E. Casey Foundation (2017). *2017 kids count data book.* Baltimore, MD: Author.

Anyon, J. (1985). "Social class and school knowledge" revisited: A reply to Ramsay. *Curriculum Inquiry, 15*(2), 207–214.

Anyon, J. (2005). What "counts" as educational policy? Notes toward a new paradigm. *Harvard Educational Review, 75*(1), 65–88.

Argyris, C., & Schön, D. A. (1974). *Theory in practice: Increasing professional effectiveness.* San Francisco: Jossey-Bass.

Armor, D., Conroy-Oseguera, P., Cox, M., King, N., McDonnell, L., Pascal, A., … Zellman, G. (1976). *Analysis of the school preferred reading programs in selected Los Angeles minority schools.* Santa Monica, CA: RAND.

Ashton, P. T., & Webb, R. B. (1986). *Making a difference: Teachers' sense of efficacy and student achievement.* New York: Longman Publishing Group.

Ashton, P. T., Webb, R. B., & Doda, N. (1982). *A study of teachers' sense of efficacy: Final report, volume 1.* Washington, DC: National Institute of Education.

Azma, S. (2013). Poverty and the developing brain: Insights from neuroimaging. *Synesis: A Journal of Science, Technology, Ethics, and Policy, 4*(1), G40–G46.

Babad, E. (2009). Teaching and nonverbal behavior in the classroom. In L. Saha & A. Dworkin (Eds.), *International Handbook of Research on Teachers and Teaching.* (Vol. 21, pp. 817–827). New York: Springer.

Babcock, E., & Ruiz De Luzuriaga, N. (2016). *Families disrupting the cycle of poverty: Coaching with an intergenerational lens.* Boston: Economic Mobility Pathways.

Bailey, J. M., & Guskey, T. R. (2000). *Implementing student-led conferences.* Thousand Oaks, CA: Corwin.

Balfanz, R., & Byrnes, V. (2012). *Chronic absenteeism: Summarizing what we know from nationally available data.* Baltimore: Johns Hopkins University Center for Social Organization of Schools. Available: http://new.every1graduates.org/wp-content /uploads/2012/05/FINALChronicAbsenteeismReport_May16.pdf

Banks, J. A. (1997). *Educating citizens in a multicultural society.* New York: Teachers College Press.

Barr, R. D., & Gibson, E. L. (2013). *Building a culture of hope: Enriching schools with optimism and opportunity.* Bloomington, IN: Solution Tree.

Barton, A. C., Tan, E., & Greenberg, D. (2017). The makerspace movement: Sites of possibilities for equitable opportunities to engage underrepresented youth in STEM. *Teachers College Record, 119*(6), 1–44.

Beady, C. H., Jr., & Hansell, S. (1981). Teacher race and expectations for student achievement. *Educational Research Journal, 18*(2), 191–206.

Beegle, D. M. (2007). *See poverty… Be the difference! Discover the missing pieces for helping people move out of poverty.* Tigard, OR: Communication Across Barriers.

Benard, B. (1997). Drawing forth resilience in all our youth: Reclaiming children and youth. *Journal of Emotional and Behavioral Problems, 6*(1), 29–32.

Benner, G. J., Nelson, J. R., Sanders, E. A., & Ralston, N. C. (2012). Behavior intervention for students with externalizing behavior problems: Primary-level standard protocol. *Exceptional Children, 78*(2), 181–198.

Benson, E. (2003). Intelligent intelligence testing. *Monitor on Psychology, 34*(2), 48–58.

Bishop, R. (2008). A culturally responsive pedagogy of relations. *The Professional Practice of Teaching, 3,* 154–171.

Bishop, R., & Berryman, M. (2006). *Culture speaks: Cultural relationships and classroom learning.* Wellington, NZ: Huia.

Bishop, R., Berryman, M., Cavanagh, T., & Teddy, L. (2007). Te Kōtahitanga Phase 3 Whānaungatanga: Establishing a culturally responsive pedagogy of relations in mainstream secondary school classrooms. *Wellington: Ministry of Education,* 81–90.

Bishop, R., Ladwig, J., & Berryman, M. (2014). The centrality of relationships for pedagogy: The Whanaungatanga thesis. *American Educational Research Journal, 51*(1), 184–214.

Black, D. S., & Fernando, R. (2014). Mindfulness training and classroom behavior among lower-income and ethnic minority elementary school children. *Journal of Child and Family Studies, 23*(7), 1242–1246.

Boaler, J. (2002). *Experiencing school mathematics: Traditional and reform approaches to teaching and their impact on student learning.* Abingdon, UK: Routledge.

Bodilly, S., Keltner, B., Purnell, S., Reichardt, R., & Schuyler, G. (1998). *Lessons from new American schools' scale-up phase: Prospects for bringing designs to multiple schools.* Santa Monica, CA: RAND.

Bondy, E., & Ross, D. D. (2008, September). The teacher as warm demander. *Educational Leadership, 66*(1), 54–58.

Bradshaw, T. K. (2006). *Theories of poverty and the practice of community development—A working paper.* Rural Poverty Research Center. Retrieved from http://www.rupri.org/Forms/WP06-05.pdf

Bransford, J., Derry, S., Berliner, D., & Hammerness, K. (2000). Theories of learning and their roles in teaching. In L. Darling-Hammond & J. Bransford (Eds.), *Preparing teachers for a changing world: What teachers should learn and be able to do.*

Brookhart, S. M. (2009, November). The many meanings of "multiple measures." *Educational Leadership, 67*(3), 6–12.

Brooks-Gunn, J., & Duncan, G. J. (1997). The effects of poverty on children. *The Future of Children, 7*(2), 55–71.

Brooks-Gunn, J., Duncan, G. J., Klebanov, P. K., & Sealand, N. (1993). Do neighborhoods influence child and adolescent development? *American Journal of Sociology, 99*(2), 353–395.

Brophy, J. E. (1982). How teachers influence what is taught and learned in classrooms. *Elementary School Journal, 83*(1), 1–13.

Brophy, J. E., & Good, T. L. (1970). Teachers' communication of differential expectations for children's classroom performance: Some behavioral data. *Journal of Educational Psychology, 61*(5), 365.

Brown, J., Miller, J., & Mitchell, J. (2006). Interrupted schooling and the acquisition of literacy: Experiences of Sudanese refugees in Victorian secondary schools. *Australian Journal of Language and Literacy, 29*(2), 150.

Brown, K. M., Benkovitz, J., Muttillo, A. J., & Urban, T. (2011). Leading schools of excellence and equity: Documenting effective strategies in closing achievement Gaps. *Teachers College Record, 113*(1), 57–96.

Bryk, A., & Schneider, B. (2002). *Trust in schools: A core resource for improvement.* New York: Russell Sage Foundation.

Buckner, J. C., Mezzacappa, E., & Beardslee, W. R. (2009). Self-regulation and its relations to adaptive functioning in low income youths. *American Journal of Orthopsychiatry, 79*(1), 19.

Budge, K. M., & Parrett, W. H. (2009). Making refugee students welcome. Retrieved October 18, 2017, from http://www.ascd.org/publications/educational-leadership/apr09/vol66/num07/Making-Refugee-Students-Welcome.aspx

Budge, K. M., & Parrett, W. H. (2016). The district's "ad-vantage" point. *School Administrator, 31*–33.

Campbell, L. & Campbell, B. (1999). *Multiple intelligences and student achievement: Success stories from six schools.* Alexandria, VA: ASCD.

Caspi, A., Taylor, A., Moffit, T. E., & Plomin, R. (2000). Neighborhood deprivation affects children's mental health: Environmental risks identified in a genetic design. *Psychological Science, 11*(4), 338–342.

Chenoweth, K. (2007). *"It's Being Done": Academic success in unexpected schools.* Cambridge, MA 02138: Harvard Education Press.

Chenoweth, K. (2009). It can be done, it's being done, and here's how. *Phi Delta Kappan, 91*(1), 38.

Children's Defense Fund (2014). *The state of America's children.* Washington, DC: Author. Retrieved from http://www.childrensdefense.org/library/state-of-americas-children/2014-soac.pdf?utm_source=2014-SOAC-PDF&utm_medium=link&utm_campaign=2014-SOAC

Cizek, G. J. (2010). *Translating standards into assessments: The opportunities and challenges of a common core.* Chapel Hill, NC: University of North Carolina.

Claro, S., Paunesku, D., & Dweck, C. (2016). Growth mindset tempers the effects of poverty on academic achievement. *Proceedings of the National Academy of Sciences, 113*(31), 8664–8668.

Coleman, J. S. (1987). Norms as social capital. In G. Radnitzky & P. Bernholz (Eds.), *Economic imperialism: The economic approach applied outside the field of economics* (pp. 133–155). New York: Paragon.

Comer, J. P. (1993). All children can learn: A developmental approach. *Holistic Education Review, 6*(1), 4–9.

Cooper, C. W. (2003). The detrimental impact of teacher bias: Lessons learned from the standpoint of African American mothers. *Teacher Education Quarterly, 30*(2), 101–116.

Cooper, D. (2013). *Raising the federal minimum wage to $10.10 would lift wages for millions and provide a modest economic boost* (Briefing Paper #371). Washington, DC: Economic Policy Institute. Retrieved from http://www.epi.org/publication/raising-federal-minimum-wage-to-1010/

Costa, A. L., & Kallick, B. (2009). *Habits of mind across the curriculum: Practical and creative strategies for teachers.* Alexandria, VA: ASCD.

Covey, S. R. (1989). *Seven habits of highly effective people: Restoring the character ethic.* New York: Simon and Schuster.

Craig, S. E. (2016). *Trauma-sensitive schools: Learning communities transforming children's lives, K–5.* New York: Teachers College Press.

Danziger, S., & Wimer, C. (2014, Special Issue). Poverty. *Pathways,* 13–18. Stanford, CA: Stanford Center on Poverty and Inequality.

Dariotis, J. K., Mirabal-Beltran, R., Cluxton-Keller, F., Gould, L. F., Greenberg, M. T., & Mendelson, T. (2016). A qualitative evaluation of student learning and skills use in a school-based mindfulness and yoga program. *Mindfulness, 7*(1), 76–89.

Darley, J. M., & Fazio, R. H. (1980). Expectancy confirmation processes arising in the social interaction sequence. *American Psychologist, 35*(10), 867.

Darling-Hammond, L. (2010). Teacher education and the American future. *Journal of Teacher Education, 61*(1–2), 35–47.

Delpit, L. (1995). *Other people's children: Cultural conflict in the classroom.* New York: New Press.

DeNavas-Walt, C., & Proctor, B. D. (2015). *Income and poverty in the United States: 2014.* Washington, DC: U.S. Census Bureau. Retrieved from http://www.census.gov/content/dam/Census/library/publications/2015/demo/p60-252.pdf

Denton, P. (2013). *The power of our words: Teacher language that helps children learn.* Turner Falls, MA: Center for Responsive Schools.

Desimone, L. M., & Long, D. (2010). Teacher effects and the achievement gap: Do teacher and teaching quality influence the achievement gap between black and white and high- and low-SES students in the early grades? *Teachers College Record, 112*(12), 3024–3073.

Dewey, J. (1915). *Democracy and education.* Democracia e Educação.

Diamond, J. B., Randolph, A., & Spillane, J. P. (2004). Teachers' expectations and sense of responsibility for student learning: The importance of race, class, and organizational habitus. *Anthropology & Education Quarterly, 35*(1), 75–98.

Dill, V. (2015, March). Homeless—And doubled up. *Educational Leadership, 72*(6), 42–47.

Domhoff, G. W. (2017). Wealth, income, and power. *Who rules America?* [Website]. Retrieved from http://www2.ucsc.edu/whorulesamerica/power/wealth.html

Dryden, J., Johnson, B., Howard, S., & McGuire, A. (1998, April). *Resiliency: A comparison of construct definitions arising from conversations with 9 year old–12 year old children and their teachers.* Paper presented at the American Educational Research Association Conference. San Diego: AERA.

Duncan, G., & Murnane, R. J. (2014). *Restoring opportunity: The crisis of inequality and the challenge for American education.* Cambridge, MA: Harvard Education Press.

Dweck, C. S. (2006). *Mindset: The new psychology of success.* New York: Random House.

Dweck, C. S. (2010). Mind-sets and equitable education. *Principal Leadership, 10*(5), 26–29.

Echevarría, J., Vogt, M., & Short, D. (2004). *Making content comprehensible for English learners: The SIOP model* (2nd ed.). Boston: Allyn and Bacon.

Edmondson, J., & Shannon, P. (1998). Reading education and poverty: Questioning the reading success equation. *Peabody Journal of Education, 73*(3–4), 104–126.

Eisenman, G., & Payne, B. D. (1997). Effects of the higher order thinking skills program on at-risk young adolescents' self-concept, reading achievement, and thinking skills. *Research in Middle Level Education Quarterly, 20*(3), 1–25.

Entwisle, D. R., Alexander, K. L., & Olson, L. S. (1998). *Children, schools and inequality. Boulder, CO: Westview Press.* Boulder, CO: Westview Press.

Fiarman, S. E. (2016). Unconscious bias: When good intentions aren't enough. *Educational Leadership, 74*(3), 10–15.

Feldman, J. (2015). *How our grading supports inequity, and what we can do about it.* SmartBrief. Retrieved from http://www.smartbrief.com/original/2015/07/how-our-grading-supports-inequity-and-what-we-can-do-about-it

Ferguson, R. (1998). Teachers' perceptions and expectations and the black-white test score gap. In C. Jencks & M. Phillips (Eds.), *The black-white test score gap* (pp. 273–317). Washington, DC: Brookings Institute.

Fine, M. (1993). "(Ap)parent involvement," *Teachers College Record, 94,* (4), 682–729.

Finn, P. J. (2009). *Literacy with an attitude: Educating working-class children in their own self-interest.* Albany: State University of New York Press.

Fogarty, R. (2009). *Brain-compatible classrooms.* Thousand Oaks, CA. Corwin.

Freire, P. (1970). *Pedagogy of the oppressed.* New York: NY: Herder & Herder.

Fullan, M. (2011). *The moral imperative realized.* Thousand Oaks, CA: Corwin.

Furco, A., & Root, S. (2010). Research demonstrates the value of service learning. *Phi Delta Kappan, 91*(5), 16–20.

Garrett, H. E. (1961). The equalitarian dogma. *Mankind Quarterly, 1,* 253–257.

Gershenson, S., Holt, S. B., & Papageorge, N. W. (2015). Who believes in me? The effect of student teacher demographic match on teacher expectations. *Economics of Education Review, 52,* 209–224.

Gibson, S., & Dembo, M. H. (1984). Teacher efficacy: A construct validation. *Journal of Educational Psychology, 76*(4), 569.

Glasmeier, A. K., & Arete, W. (2015). Living wage calculator. From http://livingwage.mit.edu

Goldhaber, D., Lavery, L., & Theobald, R. (2015). Uneven playing field? Assessing the teacher quality gap between advantaged and disadvantaged students. *Educational Researcher, 44*(5), 293–307.

Good, T. L., & Brophy, J. E. (1974). Changing teacher and student behavior: An empirical investigation. *Journal of Educational Psychology, 66*(3), 390.

Good, T. L., & Nichols, S. L. (2001). Expectancy effects in the classroom: A special focus on improving the reading performance of minority students in first-grade classrooms. *Educational Psychologist, 36*(2), 113–126.

Gorski, P. C. (2008, April). The myth of the "culture of poverty." *Educational Leadership, 65*(7), 32.

Gorski, P. C. (2012). Perceiving the problem of poverty and schooling: Deconstructing the class stereotypes that mis shape education practice and policy. *Equity & Excellence in Education, 45*(2), 302–319.

Gorski, P. C. (2013). *Reaching and teaching students in poverty: Strategies for erasing the opportunity gap.* New York: Teachers College Press.

Gregory, A., & Huang, F. (2013). It takes a village: The effects of 10th grade college-going expectations of students, parents, and teachers four years later. *American Journal of Community Psychology, 52,* 41–55.

Gregory, K., Cameron, C., & Davies, A. (2011). *Setting and using criteria.* Solution Tree Press/Building Connections Pub.

Gruenert, S., & Whitaker, T. (2015). *School culture rewired: How to define, assess, and transform it.* Alexandria, VA: ASCD.

Guskey, T. R. (1982). The effects of change in instructional effectiveness on the relationship of teacher expectations and student achievement. *Journal of Educational Research, 75*(6), 345–349.

Guskey, T. R. (1986). Staff development and the process of teacher change. *Educational Researcher, 15*(5), 5–12.

Guskey, T. R. (1988). Teacher efficacy, self-concept, and attitudes toward the implementation of instructional innovation. *Teaching and Teacher Education, 4*(1), 63–69.

Guskey, T. R. (2000). Grading policies that work against standards … and how to fix them. *NASSP Bulletin, 84*(620), 20–29.

Guskey, T. R., & Bailey, J. M. (2001). *Developing grading and reporting systems for student learning.* Thousand Oaks, CA: Corwin.

Guskey, T. R., & Passaro, P. D. (1994). Teacher efficacy: A study of construct dimensions. *American Educational Research Journal, 31*(3), 627–643.

Guyton, E. (2000). Social justice in teacher education. *The Educational Forum, 64*(2), 108–114.

Haberman, M. (1991). The pedagogy of poverty versus good teaching. *Phi Delta Kappan, 73*(4), 290–294.

Haberman, M. (1995). *Star teachers of children in poverty.* West Lafayette, IN: Kappa Delta Pi.

Haberman, M. (1996). Selecting and preparing culturally competent teachers for urban schools. In J. Silusa (Ed.), *Handbook of research on teacher education* (pp. 747–760). New York: Macmillan.

Haberman, M. (2012). The myth of the "fully qualified" bright young teacher. *American Behavioral Scientist, 56*(7), 926–940.

Hall, P., & Simeral, A. (2015). *Teach, reflect, learn: Building your capacity for success in the classroom.* Alexandria, VA: ASCD.

Harris, M. J., & Rosenthal, R. (1985). Mediation of interpersonal expectancy effects: 31 meta-analyses. *Psychological Bulletin, 97*, 363–386.

Hattie, J. (2009). *Visible learning: A synthesis of over 800 meta-analyses relating to achievement.* Abingdon, UK: Routledge.

Herrnstein, R. J., & Murray, C. (1994). *The bell curve: Intelligence and class structure in American life.* New York: Free Press.

Hilfiker, D. (2002). *Urban injustice: How ghettos happen.* New York: Seven Stories Press.

Hinton, C. (n.d.). Neuroscience research backs up Ned's Gr8 8. Available: http://www.whatkidscando.org/featurestories/2013/01_how_youth_learn

Hinton, C., Fischer, K. W., & Glennon, C. (2012). *Mind, brain, and education.* Boston: Jobs for the Future.

Hispanic Heritage Foundation. (2015). *Taking the pulse of the high school student experience in America. Research findings: Phase one: Access to technology.*

Honigsfeld, A., & Dunn, R. (2009). *Differentiating instruction for at-risk students: What to do and how to do it.* Lanham, MD: Rowman & Littlefield Education.

Hyerle, D. (2009). *Visual tools for transforming information into knowledge.* Thousand Oaks, CA: Corwin.

Ingraham, C. (2015). If you thought income inequality was bad, get a load of wealth inequality. [Wonkblog]. Retrieved from https://www.washingtonpost.com/news/wonk/wp/2015/05/21/the-top-10-of-americans-own-76-of-the-stuff-and-its-dragging-our-economy-down/?utm_term=.17f246d1c2a1.

Jensen, A. R. (1969). How much can we boost IQ and scholastic achievement? *Harvard Educational Review, 39*, 1–123.

Jensen, A. R. (1973). *Educability and group differences*. New York: Harper & Row.

Jensen, E. (2009). *Teaching with poverty in mind: What being poor does to kids' brains and what schools can do about it*. Alexandria, VA: ASCD.

Johannessen, L. R. (2004). Helping "struggling" students achieve success. *Journal of Adolescent and Adult Literacy, 47*(8), 638–647.

Johnson, B. (2008). Teacher-student relationships which promote resilience at school: A micro-level analysis of students' views. *British Journal of Guidance and Counseling, 36*(4), 385–398.

Johnston, P. H. (2004). *Choice words: How our language affects children's learning*. Portland, ME: Stenhouse.

Johnston, P. H. (2012). *Opening minds: Using language to change lives*. Portland, ME: Stenhouse.

Jordan, G. (2004). The causes of poverty—cultural vs. structural: Can there be a synthesis? *Perspectives in Public Affairs, 1*, 18–34.

Kameenui, E. J., & Carnine, D. W. (1998). *Effective teaching strategies that accommodate diverse learners*. Des Moines: Prentice-Hall.

Keller, J., & McDade, K. (2000). Attitudes of low-income parents toward seeking help with parenting: Implications for practice. *Child Welfare, 79*(3), 285.

Kinsley, C. W. (1997). Service-learning: A process to connect learning and living. *NASSP Bulletin, 81*(591), 1–7.

Kleinfeld, J. (1975). Effective teachers of Eskimo and Indian students. *School Review, 83*(2), 301–344.

Knapp, M. S. (1984). *The economics of social care*. New York: Macmillan.

Knapp, M. S., & Adelman, N (1995). *Teaching for meaning in high-poverty classrooms*. New York: Teachers College Press.

Knapp, M. S., Shields, P. M., & Turnbull, B. J. (1995). Academic challenge in high-poverty classrooms. *Phi Delta Kappan, 76*(10), 770.

Kneebone, E., & Berube, A. (2013). *Confronting suburban poverty in America*. Brookings Institution Press.

Knowles, M. S. (1980). *The modern practice of adult education: From pedagogy to andragogy* (Rev. ed.). New York: Adult Education Company.

Koch, J., & Mettler, S. (2012). Who perceives government's role in their lives? Assessing the impact of social policy on visibility. Retrieved from https://ash.harvard.edu/event/who-perceives-governments-role-their-lives

Kolb, D. A. (1984). *Experiential learning: Experience as the source of learning and development*. Upper Saddle River, NJ: Prentice Hall.

Kozol, J. (1991). *Savage inequalities: Children in America's schools*. New York: Crown.

Kralovec, E., & Buell, J. (2000). *The end of homework: How homework disrupts families, overburdens children, and limits learning*. Boston: Beacon Press.

Ladson-Billings, G. (1994). *The dreamkeepers: Successful schooling for African-American students*. San Francisco: Jossey-Bass.

Ladson-Billings, G. (2009). *The dreamkeepers: Successful teachers of African American children* (2nd ed.). San Francisco: Jossey-Bass.

Lalas, J. (2007). Teaching for social justice in multicultural urban schools: Conceptualization and classroom implication. *Multicultural Education, 14*(3), 17.

Langer, J. (2001). Beating the odds: Teaching middle and secondary school students to read and write well. *American Educational Research Journal, 38*, 837–880.

Lareau, A. (1987). Social class differences in family-school relationships: The importance of cultural capital. *Sociology of Education, 60*(2), 73–85.

Larkin, D. (2012). Using the conceptual change model of learning as an analytic tool in researching teacher preparation for student diversity. *Teachers College Record, 114*(8), 1–35.

Larson, C. L., & Ovando, C. (2001). *The color of bureaucracy: The politics of equity in multicultural school communities.* Florence, KY: Taylor and Francis.

Lindsey, R. B., Karns, M. S., & Myatt, K. (2010). *Culturally proficient education: An asset-based response to conditions of poverty.* Thousand Oaks, CA: Corwin.

Lindt, S. F., & Miller, S. C. (2017). Movement and learning in elementary school. *Phi Delta Kappan, 98*(7), 34–37.

Lott, B. (2001). Low-income parents and the public schools. *Journal of Social Issues, 57*(2), 247–259.

Lott, B. (2003). Recognizing and welcoming the standpoint of low-income parents in the public schools. *Journal of Educational and Psychological Consultation, 14*(1), 91–104.

Luthar, S. S., & Becker, B. E. (2002). Privileged but pressured? A study of affluent youth. *Child Development, 73*(5), 1593–1610.

Lynn, R., & Vanhanen, T. (2006). *IQ and global inequity.* Augusta, GA: Washington Summit Publishers.

Mani, A., Mullainathan, S., Shafir, E., & Zhao, J. (2013). Poverty impedes cognitive function. *Science, 341*(6149), 976–980.

Marzano, R. J. (2000). *Transforming classroom grading.* Alexandria, VA: ASCD.

Mattingly, D. J., Prislin, R., McKenzie, T. L., Rodriguez, J. L., & Kayzar, B. (2002). Evaluating evaluations: The case of parent involvement programs. *Review of Educational Research, 72*(4), 549–576.

McAllister, G., & Irvine, J. J. (2002). The role of empathy in teaching culturally diverse students: A qualitative study of teachers' beliefs. *Journal of Teacher Education, 53*(5), 433–443.

McKown, C., & Weinstein, R. S. (2002). Modeling the role of child ethnicity and gender in children's differential response to teacher expectations. *Journal of Applied Social Psychology, 32*(1), 159–184.

McMillan, J. H. (2001). Secondary teachers' classroom assessment and grading practices. *Educational Measurement: Issues and Practice, 20*(1), 20–32.

Miller, A. (2016, July 8). Do no harm: Flexible and smart grading practices. Edutopia. Retrieved from https://www.edutopia.org/blog/do-no-harm-flexible-smart-grading-andrew-miller

Milner, H. R., IV (2015). *Rac(e)ing to class: Confronting poverty and race in schools and classrooms.* Cambridge, MA: Harvard Education Press.

Moll, L. C., Amanti, C., Neff, D., & Gonzalez, N. (1992). Funds of knowledge for teaching: Using a qualitative approach to connect homes and classrooms. *Theory into Practice, 31*(2), 132–141.

National Center for Homeless Education. (2016). *Federal Data Summary: School Years 2012–2013 to 2014–2015.* Greensboro, NC: UNC. Retrieved from https://nche.ed.gov/downloads/data-comp-1213-1415.pdf

National Institutes of Health. (2012, August 28). Stresses of poverty may impair learning ability in young children. Author. Retrieved from https://www.nih.gov/news-events/news-releases/stresses-poverty-may-impair-learning-ability-young-children

Neason, A. (2017). Does homework help? *ASCD: Education Update, 59*(1).

Neuman, S. B. (2008). *Educating the other America.* Baltimore: Brookes.

Newmann, F., Bryk, A. S., & Nagaoka, J. K. (2001). *Improving Chicago's schools: Authentic intellectual work and standardized tests: Conflict or coexistence?* Chicago: Consortium on Chicago School Research.

Nichols, S. L., & Good, T. (2004) *America's teenagers—myths and realities: Media images, schooling, and the social costs of careless indifference.* New York: Routledge.

Noble, K. G., Houston, S. M., Brito, N. H., Bartsch, H., Kan, E., Kuperman, J. M., ... Sowell, E. R. (2015). Family income, parental education and brain structure in children and adolescents. *Nature Neuroscience, 18*(5), 773–778.

Noddings, N. (2010). Moral education in an age of globalization. *Educational Philosophy and Theory, 42*(4), 390 396.

OECD. (2011). *An overview of growing income inequalities in OECD countries: Main findings.* Paris: Author.

OECD. (2015). *In it together: Why less inequality benefits all.* Paris: Author.

Okonofua, J. A., Paunesku, D., & Walton, G. M. (2016). Brief intervention to encourage empathic discipline cuts suspension rates in half among adolescents. *Proceedings of the National Academy of Sciences, 113*(19). Retrieved from www.pnas.org/cgi/doi/10.1073/pnas.1523698113

Ornelles, C. (2007). Providing classroom-based intervention to at-risk students to support their academic engagement and interactions with peers. *Preventing School Failure: Alternative Education for Children and Youth, 51*(4), 3–12.

Palinscar, A., & Brown, A. (1985). Reciprocal teaching: Activities to promote "reading with your mind." In T. L. Harris & E. J. Cooper (Eds.), *Reading, thinking, and concept development: Strategies for the classroom* (pp. 299–310). New York: College Board.

Palmer, P. (2007). *The courage to teach: Exploring the inner landscape of a teacher's life.* San Francisco: Jossey-Bass.

Parker, L., & Shapiro, J. P. (1993). The context of educational administration and social class. In C. A. Capper (Ed.), *Educational administration in a pluralistic society* (pp. 36–65). Albany: State University of New York Press.

Parrett, W. H., & Budge, K. M. (2009). Tough questions for tough times. *Educational Leadership, 67*(2), 1–5.

Parrett, W. H., & Budge, K. (2012). *Turning high-poverty schools into high performing schools.* Alexandria, VA: ASCD.

Pellegrini, A. D., & Bohn, C. M. (2005). The role of recess in children's cognitive performance and school adjustment. *Educational Researcher, 34*(1), 13–19.

Pijanowski, L. (2011, November). The case of the illogical grades. *Educational Leadership, 69*(3). Available: http://www.ascd.org/publications/educational-leadership/nov11/vol69/num03/The-Case-of-the-Illogical-Grades.aspx

Pogrow, S. (2005). HOTS revisited: A thinking development approach to reducing the learning gap after grade 3. *Phi Delta Kappan, 87*(1), 64–75.

Pogrow, S. (2006). The Bermuda Triangle of American education: Pure traditionalism, pure progressivism, and good intentions. *Phi Delta Kappan, 88*(2), 142–150.

Quaglia, R. J., & Fox, K. M. (2003). *Student aspirations: Eight conditions that make a difference*. Champaign, IL: Research Press.

Quaglia, R. J., Fox, K. M., & Corso, M. J. (2010, November). Got opportunity? *Educational Leadership*, *68*(3). Available: http://www.ascd.org/publications/educational-leadership/nov10/vol68/num03/Got-Opportunity%C2%A2.aspx

Rank, M. R. (2005). *One nation, underprivileged: Why American poverty affects us all*. New York: Oxford University Press.

Rank, M. R. (2006). Toward a new understanding of American poverty. *Washington University Journal of Law and Policy*, *20*, 16–51.

Reardon, S. (2015, March 30). Poverty shrinks brains from birth. *Nature International Weekly Journal of Science*. Retrieved from http://www.nature.com/news/poverty-shrinks-brains-from-birth-1.17227

Redding, S. (2013). *Through the student's eyes: A perspective on personalized learning and practice guide for teachers*. Philadelphia: Center on Innovations in Learning.

Reeves, D. B. (2004). The case against zero. *Phi Delta Kappan*, *86*(4), 324–325.

Reeves, D. B. (2008, February). Leading to change/Effective grading practices. *Educational Leadership*, *65*(5), 85–87.

Reeves, D. B. (2016) *Elements of grading: A guide to effective practice*. Bloomington, IN: Solution Tree.

Reeves, R. (2014). *Saving Horatio Alger: Equality, opportunity, and the American dream*. Washington, DC: Brookings Institution Press.

Rist, R. C. (1970). Student social class and teacher expectations: The self-fulfilling prophecy in ghetto education. *Harvard Educational Review*, *40*(3), 411–451.

Rist, R. C. (1979). On the means of knowing: Qualitative research in education. *New York University Education Quarterly*, *10*(4), 17–21.

Rist, R. C. (2000). HER classic reprint: Student social class and teacher expectations: The self-fulfilling prophecy in ghetto education. *Harvard Educational Review*, *70*(3), 257–302.

Roberts, B., Povich, D., & Mather, M. (2013). Low-income working families: The growing economic gap. *Working Poor Families Project*, *301*(3).

Robinson, J. G. (2007). Presence and persistence: Poverty ideology and inner-city teaching. *Urban Review*, *39*(5), 541–565.

Rockwell, S. (2007). Working smarter, not harder: Reaching the tough to teach: Part I: Prior knowledge and concept development. *Kappa Delta Pi Record*, *44*(1), 8–12.

Rogers, C. R. (1957). The necessary and sufficient conditions of therapeutic personality change. *Journal of Consulting Psychology*, *21*, 95–103.

Rogers, J., & Mirra, N. (2014). *It's about time: Learning time and educational opportunity in California high schools*. Los Angeles: UCLA's Institute for Democracy, Education, and Access.

Rosenthal, R. (1974). *On the social psychology of the self-fulfilling prophecy: Further evidence for Pygmalion effects and their mediating mechanisms*. New York: MSS Modular Publications.

Rosenthal, R., & Jacobson, L. (1968). Pygmalion in the classroom. *Urban Review*, *3*(1), 16–20.

Rothstein, R. (2004, November). The achievement gap: A broader picture. *Educational Leadership*, *62*(3), 40–43.

Routman, R. (2014). *Read, write, lead: Breakthrough strategies for schoolwide literacy success*. Alexandria, VA: ASCD.

Rubie-Davies, C. M. (2015). High and low expectation teachers: The importance of the teacher factor. In S. Trusz & P. Babel, (Eds.), *Interpersonal and Intrapersonal Expectancies* (Ch. 18). New York: Routledge.

Rubie-Davies, C., Hattie, J., & Hamilton, R. (2006). Expecting the best for students: Teacher expectations and academic outcomes. *British Journal of Educational Psychology, 76*(3), 429–444.

Rubie-Davies, C. M. (2015). High and low expectation teachers: The importance of the teacher factor. In *Expectancies for students and others: What we know from 55 years of research*. Psychology Press.

Rubie-Davies, C. M., Peterson, E. R., Sibley, C. G., & Rosenthal, R. (2015). A teacher expectation intervention: Modelling the practices of high expectation teachers. *Contemporary Educational Psychology, 40*, 72–85.

Rushton, J. P. (2000). *Race, evolution, and behavior: A life history perspective* (3rd ed.). Port Huron, MI: Charles Darwin Research Institute.

Sanburn, J. (2013). The rise of suburban poverty in America. Accessed: http://time.com/3060122/poverty-america-suburbs-brookings

Santoro, D. A. (2011). Good teaching in difficult times: Demoralization in the pursuit of good work. *American Journal of Education, 118*(1), 1–23.

Scales, P. (2013). *Teaching in the lifelong learning sector.* (2nd ed.). Berkshire, England: Open University Press.

Schlichter, C., Hobbs, D., & Crump, D. (1988, April). Extending talents unlimited to secondary schools. *Educational Leadership, 45*(7), 36–40.

Schön, D. A. (1983). *The reflective practitioner: How professionals think in action.* New York: Basic Books.

Semega, J., Fontenot, K., & Kollar, M. (2017). *Income and poverty in the United States: 2016*. U. S. Census Bureau, Current Populations Report. Washington, CD: U. S. Government Printing Office.

Sheridan, K., Halverson, E. R., Litts, B., Brahms, L., Jacobs-Priebe, L., & Owens, T. (2014). Learning in the making: A comparative case study of three makerspaces. *Harvard Educational Review, 84*(4), 505–531.

Sherman, A., Greenstein, R., & Ruffing, K. (2012, February 11). Contrary to "entitlement society" rhetoric, over nine-tenths of entitlement benefits go to elderly, disabled, or working households. *Center on Budget and Policy Priorities.* Retrieved from http://www.cbpp.org/research/contrary-to-entitlement-society-rhetoric-over-nine-tenths-of-entitlement-benefits-go-to

Shuey, A. M. (1958). *The testing of negro intelligence.* Lynchburg, VA: J. P. Bell.

Shuey, A. M. (1966). *The testing of negro intelligence* (2nd ed.). New York: Social Science Press.

Shyamalan, M. N. (2013). *I got schooled: The unlikely story of how a moonlighting movie maker learned the five keys to closing America's education gap.* New York: Simon and Schuster.

Sibley, B. A., & Etnier, L. (2003). The relationship between physical activity and cognition in children: A meta-analysis. *Pediatric Exercise Science, 15*(3), 243–256.

Singer, T. W. (2014). *Opening doors to equity: A practical guide to observation-based professional learning.* Thousand Oaks, CA: Corwin.

Smith, G. A., & Sobel, D. (2010). *Place- and community-based education in schools*. New York: Routledge.

Smylie, M. A. (1988). The enhancement function of staff development: Organizational and psychological antecedents to individual teacher change. *American Educational Research Journal, 25*(1), 1–30.

Solomon, D., Battistich, V., & Hom, A. (1996). Teacher beliefs and practices in schools serving communities that differ in socioeconomic level. *Journal of Experimental Education, 64*(4), 327–347.

Southern Education Foundation. (2015). *A new majority research bulletin: Low income students now a majority in the nation's public schools*. Retrieved from http://www. southerneducation.org/Our-Strategies/Research-and-Publications/New-Majority -Diverse-Majority-Report-Series/A-New-Majority-2015-Update-Low-Income -Students-Now

Sparks, S. D. (2016, July 13). One key to reducing school suspension: A little respect. *Education Week*. Retrieved from http://www.edweek.org/ew/articles/2016/07/13/one -key-to-reducing-school-suspension-a.html

Steele, C. M., & Aronson, J. (1995). Stereotype threat and the intellectual test performance of African Americans. *Journal of Personality and Social Psychology, 69*(5), 797.

Steenland, S. (2013, February 13). Working full time and still poor. *Center for American Progress*. Retrieved from https://www.americanprogress.org/issues/religion /news/2013/02/20/53929/working-full-time-and-still-poor/

Stride, Y., & Cutcher, A. (2015). Manifesting resilience in the secondary school: An investigation of the relationship dynamic in visual arts classrooms. *International Journal of Education and the Arts, 16*(11).

Suitts, S. (2015). A new majority research bulletin: Low income students now a majority in the nation's public schools. Retrieved from http://www.southerneducation.org /Our-Strategies/Research-and-Publications/New-Majority-Diverse-Majority -Report-Series/A-New-Majority-2015-Update-Low-Income-Students-Now

Toder, E., Baneman, D., & Center, U. B. T. . (2012). *Distributional effects of individual income tax expenditures: An update*. Washington, DC: Urban-Brookings Tax Policy Center.

Tomlinson, C. A., Brighton, C., Hertberg, H., Callahan, C., Moon, T. R., Brimijoin, K., & Reynolds, T. (2003). Differentiating instruction in response to student readiness, interest, and learning profile in academically diverse classrooms: A review of literature. *Journal for the Education of the Gifted, 27*(2/3), 119–145.

Tschannen-Moran, H., Hoy, A. W., & Hoy, W. K. (1998). Teacher efficacy: Its meaning and measure. *Review of Educational Research, 68*(2), 202–248.

Tucker-Drob, E. M., & Bates, T. C. (2016). Large cross-national differences in gene x socioeconomic status interaction on intelligence. *Psychological Science, 27*(2), 138–149.

Ullucci, K., & Howard, T. (2015). Pathologizing the poor: Implications for preparing teachers to work in high-poverty schools. *Urban Education, 50*(2), 170–193.

U. S. Bureau of Labor Statistics. (2014). *A profile of the working poor, 2012*. (Report No. 1047). Washington, DC: Author. Retrieved from https://www.bls.gov/opub/reports /working-poor/archive/workingpoor_2012.pdf

Valencia, R. R. (2010). *Dismantling contemporary deficit thinking: Educational thought and practice*. New York: Routledge.

Valentine, C. A. (1968). *Culture and poverty: Critique and counter-proposals.* Chicago: University of Chicago Press.

Valentine, C. A. (1969). Culture and poverty: Critique and counter-proposals. *Current Anthropology, 10*(2/3), 181–201.

Valenzuela, A. (1999). *Subtractive schooling: US–Mexican youth and the politics of caring.* New York: State University of New York Press.

Vatterott, C. (2009). *Rethinking homework: Best practices that support diverse needs.* Alexandria, VA: ASCD.

Wagner, T., & Dintersmith, T. (2015). *Most likely to succeed: Preparing our kids for the innovation era.* New York: Simon and Schuster.

Walsh, J. (1999). The role of area-based programmes in tackling poverty. In D. G. Pringle, J. Walsh, and M. Hennessy (Eds.), *Poor people, poor place: A geography of poverty and deprivation in Ireland* (pp. 279–312). Dublin: Oak Tree Press.

Ware, F. (2006). Warm demander pedagogy: Culturally responsive teaching that supports a culture of achievement for African American students. *Urban Education, 41*(4), 427–456.

Weinstein, R. S. (2002). *Reaching higher: The power of expectations in schooling.* Cambridge, MA: Harvard University Press.

Weinstein, R. S., Soulé, C. R., Collins, F., Cone, J., Mehlhorn, M., & Sintontacchi, K. (1991). Expectations and high school change: Teacher-researcher collaboration to prevent school failure. *American Journal of Community Psychology, 19*(3), 333–363.

Wenger, E. (n.d.). Communities of practice: A brief introduction. Retrieved from http://www.ewenger.com/theory/index.htm

Wenger, E. (1998). Communities of practice: Learning as a social system. *Systems Thinker, 9*(5), 2–3.

Williams, D. T. (2003, November). Rural routes to success. *Educational Leadership, 61*(3), 66–70.

Williamson, M. (1992). *A return to love.* New York, NY: HarperCollins.

Wilson, W. J. (2009). *More than just race: Being black and poor in the inner city.* New York: W. W. Norton.

Wong, O. K. (2011). *High-poverty, high-performing schools: Foundations for real student success.* R&L Education.

Wood, D., Kurtz-Costes, B., & Copping, K. E. (2011). Gender differences in motivational pathways to college for middle class African American youths. *Developmental Psychology, 47*, 961–968.

Wormeli, R. (2006). *Fair isn't always equal: Assessing and grading in the differentiated classroom.* Portland, ME: Stenhouse.

Yentel, D., Aurand, A., Emmanuel, D., Errico, E., Leong, G. M., & Rodrigues, K. (2016). *Out of reach 2016.* National Low Income Housing Coalition. Retrieved from http://nlihc.org/sites/default/files/oor/OOR_2016_0.pdf

INDEX

Note: The letter *f* following a page number denotes a figure.

ABOUT THE AUTHORS

Kathleen M. Budge brings a blend of 26 years of practical experience as a teacher and administrator combined with more than a decade of work dedicated to bridging the gap between the university and the teaching profession. She is an associate professor of Educational Leadership and chair of the Curriculum, Instruction, and Foundational Studies Department at Boise State University, where her research focuses on poverty, rural education, school improvement, and leadership development. Budge is coauthor (with William Parrett) of the 2012 award-winning book *Turning High-Poverty Schools into High-Performing Schools,* and the video series, *Disrupting Poverty in Elementary and Secondary Classrooms.* She has conducted numerous presentations at international, national, and state conferences and served as guest speaker for webinars, podcasts, and symposiums related to the topic of poverty and the "whole child." Budge's consultancies include state departments, boards of education, education associations, state and regional service providers, and schools in 15 states and 3 nations. She earned her doctorate from the University of Washington in 2005. Budge continues to maintain that her most important and significant work has been teaching first graders to read. Contact her at kathleenbudge@boisestate.edu or follow her on Twitter at @KathleenBudge.

William H. Parrett has received international recognition for his work in school improvement related to children and adolescents who live in poverty. He has coauthored nine books; three recent books are best sellers. The award-winning *Turning High-Poverty Schools into High-Performing Schools*, coauthored with Kathleen Budge, has provided a Framework for Action that has been adopted throughout the United States to guide lasting improvement and student success in high-poverty schools. As director of the Boise State University Center for School Improvement and Policy Studies (since 1996), Parrett coordinates funded projects and school improvement initiatives that currently exceed $5 million a year and in excess of $70 million over the past 21 years. He is a frequent speaker at international and national events and his work with state and regional educational organizations, districts, and schools spans 44 states and 10 nations. Throughout his career, Parrett has worked to improve the educational achievement of all children and youth, particularly those less advantaged. These efforts have positively affected the lives of thousands of young people, many of whom live in poverty. Contact Parrett by e-mail at wparret@boisestate.edu or follow him on Twitter at @WHParrett.

Related ASCD Resources: Poverty

At the time of publication, the following resources were available (ASCD stock numbers in parentheses). For up-to-date information about ASCD resources, go to www.ascd.org. You can search the complete archives of *Educational Leadership* at www.ascd.org/el.

CD-ROMs

Disrupting Poverty in the Elementary School (DVD) with William H. Parrett and Kathleen M. Budge (#616044)

Disrupting Poverty in the Secondary School (DVD) with William H. Parrett and Kathleen M. Budge (#616071)

Print Products

Engaging Students with Poverty in Mind: Practical Strategies for Raising Achievement by Eric Jensen (#113001)

Turning High-Poverty Schools into High-Performing Schools by William H. Parrett and Kathleen M. Budge (#109003)

Aim High, Achieve More: How to Transform Urban Schools Through Fearless Leadership by Yvette Jackson and *Veronica McDermott* (#112015)

Creating the Opportunity to Learn: Moving from Research to Practice to Close the Achievement Gap by A. Wade Boykin & Pedro Noguera (#107016)

Create Success! Unlocking the Potential of Urban Students by Kadhir Rajagopal (#111022)

Raising Black Students' Achievement Through Culturally Responsive Teaching by Johnnie McKinley (#110004)

Teaching with Poverty in Mind: What Being Poor Does to Kids' Brains and What Schools Can Do About It by Eric Jensen (#109074)

ASCD EDge® Group

Exchange ideas and connect with other educators interested in poverty on the social networking site ASCD EDge at http://ascdedge.ascd.org/.

ASCD myTeachSource®

Download resources from a professional learning platform with hundreds of research-based best practices and tools, including video and reproducibles, for your classroom at http://myteachsource.ascd.org/.

For more information, send an e-mail to member@ascd.org; call 1-800-933-2723 or 703-578-9600; send a fax to 703-575-5400; or write to Information Services, ASCD, 1703 N. Beauregard St., Alexandria, VA 22311-1714 USA.